A Life in
POSTCARDS

A Life in
POSTCARDS

Melosina Lenox-Conyngham

edited by
SOPHIA GRENE

THE LILLIPUT PRESS
DUBLIN

First published 2013 by
THE LILLIPUT PRESS
62–63 Sitric Road, Arbour Hill
Dublin 7, Ireland
www.lilliputpress.ie

ISBN 978 1 84351 401 5

3 5 7 9 10 8 6 4 2

A CIP record for this title is available
from The British Library.

Set in 11 on 14.8pt Bembo by Marsha Swan
Printed in Spain by GraphyCems

Contents

VI: PERSONAL

Dropping Frozen from the Bough

Note on the Text

Most of the essays, which are here collected for the first time, were broadcast on *Sunday Miscellany* (to which Melosina Lenox-Conyngham was a regular contributor from the mid 1980s) or appeared in *The Irish Times* either in 'An Irishwoman's Diary' or in the travel section of the magazine from 2004 to 2011, the year of her death. They have been lightly edited to remove anomalies and repetitions, while preserving their distinctive tone as the occasional pieces they were.

Remembering Melo

A postcard with an unfamiliar stamp was usually covered in the familiar, flamboyantly spiky handwriting, often just a few words taking up all the space to tell you that the food in Baku was disgusting or that cycling round the Netherlands was harder than it looked.

Throughout her life, Melo gallantly flung herself at adventure like a knight of King Arthur's Round Table going in search of a quest purely in order to return and tell the admiring stay-at-homes about it. Even less challenging trips, such as walks up the Nore Valley, would somehow turn into adventures – although Inca, her dog in later life, frequently made that inevitable as she wreaked havoc among local livestock.

Melo's reports from these forays, as well as of her daily life in Kilkenny, were often similar in effect to her postcards: one was given a snapshot of an exciting moment, usually with some humour attached, and over time one built up a picture of her travels and her life, without ever getting a comprehensive narrative; a story-arc in the jargon of a television series.

Her undeniable courage was shot through with a surprising timidity, a wholly unjustified lack of self-confidence about certain things. Although fearless about accosting total strangers in a way most people would find terrifying, she was nervous of swimming in the sea. Although confident she knew precisely how to improve the manners and behaviour of a young niece or nephew, she was diffident about her writing and refrained from taking it seriously until her middle years.

As readers of this book will discover, this was a huge pity. Melo's writing is fluent and distinctive, evoking her voice with great fidelity for anyone who knew her. The format that suited her best was very like the postcard: the brief column for a newspaper or radio show, often telling a personal story but equally frequently framing some well-researched history in an anecdotal form, making us feel her subject.

Although born in Ceylon (now Sri Lanka) in 1941 and brought up in County Louth, Melo was firmly rooted in the Kilkenny countryside where she was based for most of her adult life. Lavistown Cottage, known as 'Bunnikins' to the family after a children's china pattern, was always welcoming, if freezing cold. Her uncle, the essayist Hubert Butler, lived a few miles away in Maidenhall, the house where he and Melo's mother grew up, until his death in 1990. It was Hubert who set up the Butler Society, a genealogical society devoted to the history and present state of the Butler family, from Kilkenny Castle, ancient seat of the Butlers, to German von Butlars, not actually relations but still interested in the family.

Her combination of generosity, familial affection, curiosity and intrepidity was useful, nay vital, to her as secretary of the Butler Society. For much of the year, this role was purely an administrative one, but once every three years it took over her life, and often that of at least one other family member, as she organized the Butler Rally.

I was commandeered as helper on a couple of occasions. The first, the Butler Rally to Birr and Portumna, led to my initial attempt at journalism in a report for *The Journal of the Butler Society*. Those interested in the details of the event can read for themselves in their back issues of that publication – III:2 (1988–9); I recall only the dismal weather, the toy museum at Birr Castle, and Melo's constant orders. These were sometimes errands, but more often commands to make sure that somebody was okay, that an elderly Butler could make it up the steps, or that quiet Butlers (they do exist) were getting their fair share of sandwiches at lunch.

Although my fourteen-year-old self muttered rebelliously at times, particularly when Melo ordered me to go and 'be nice to the grizzly girl' who was a little bit older and a lot cooler than I was, and was only grizzly because of being stuck with such an uncool day out that my niceness could in no way alleviate, I enjoyed feeling useful and competent, something that no other adult made me feel at that time.

This was one of Melo's gifts: although not conventionally 'good with children', her ability to set them tasks within their powers but that clearly needed doing was a great strength.

As aunt to grown-ups, her impact was different. She was always interested in and impressed by one's achievements, although she did prefer one to do things that made good dinner-party stories. For me, this acted as a spur to live a more interesting life, always secure in the knowledge that even if I did have a very dull nine-to-five job, it would be made to sound bizarre and adventurous when filtered through Melo's anecdotal delivery.

This was no attempt at living vicariously through nephews and nieces, however. Melo lived up to her own standards of adventure, from trips to Yemen, to the Anglo-Irish New Age weekend with Sister Imelda, dancing on the lawn to greet the sunrise. It was a joy and a privilege to have Melo as an aunt. We miss her.

Most of the essays in this book were written for the RTÉ radio programme *Sunday Miscellany* or for *The Irish Times*, where they appeared in the 'Irishwoman's Diary' column or the magazine. To give the book coherence, I have organized the material into thematic sections with individual introductions by friends and relations. I am most grateful to all those who contributed to bringing together this rich and varied anthology of her work. I owe a special debt of gratitude to the committee of the Butler Society for financial support for the book and in particular to John Kirwan who was always such a good friend to Melo.

Sophia Grene
2013

I

CHILDHOOD

A Niece's View

LUCINDA LENOX-CONYNGHAM

Melo was an Aunt with a capital A – when she wrote about her own aunts, they too were Aunts with a capital A – and Aunts featured in many of her writings about her childhood. This was, of course, partly due to the fact that many of her school holidays were spent in Ireland with her Aunt Laura in County Cork, as it was not always either possible or feasible to travel back to Ceylon (Sri Lanka).

Her other Aunts, Peggy, Noreen and Cicely, all seemed to have been both inspiring and somewhat terrifying at times. The Aunt was a very important influence in her upbringing and perhaps this is why Auntie Melo therefore felt, quite rightly, that she had an important role to play in the lives of her nieces and nephews.

The Aunt had extremely strict ideas about the upbringing of children, which she endeavoured to pass on to us. This was not always a great success as our generation was not quite so good at being seen and not heard as hers had been, certainly not as well behaved as Melo would have liked.

Trying to ensure we had impeccable table manners, extensive vocabulary and were extremely well read was just a part of her mission. She did *her absolute best to encourage us to lead interesting lives and was very keen for us to have adventures. The few times in my life I have been in real or at least perceived danger, the biggest consolation was knowing just how delighted Melo was going to be when I told her all about it. This was a strong motivating force behind my survival. We didn't exactly have to sing for our supper, but we were certainly expected to come up with a good tale or two if we wanted to find favour with this particular Aunt. Likewise, she always felt it her duty to come up with a good story in return, which is quite possibly why she wrote so much.*

Reading these extracts from her writings about her childhood takes me back to my own. I remember sitting open-mouthed with wonder as my Aunt told stories of elephants, hummingbirds, tea planters, coolies and what seemed an extraordinarily exotic world. A whole new vocabulary had to be learned just to understand what the Aunt was talking about. It seemed to be a magical existence and very far from the endless rain and chilblains that dominated my early years. Just as in her writing, the stories she told made these places come alive. Kandy, Wattegodde, the Hill School and Colombo are all places I have never been to yet feel I could accurately describe thanks to Melo's vivid descriptions. She had a great gift for writing exactly as she spoke.

She had many stories to tell of her time at boarding school, which sounded impossibly harsh. The way she described it made it seem like a place designed to make young girls miserable and where the judgment of the other girls seemed to be especially cruel. In fact, there were very few redeeming factors at all in this educational establishment. It made my own boarding school more bearable by comparison.

I couldn't imagine what it would be like to only see one's parents every two years, although by the time I was a teenager this idea became more attractive. Her stories of this period in her life portray a very different era where social etiquette and doing and saying the right thing was of the utmost importance. I find them a fascinating insight into the education of women in the middle of the last century. Hers was perhaps the last generation educated to be 'wives' rather than to have a career, yet there was a sense that they needed to do something useful for a few years so that they'd acquire skills other than flower arranging and cookery.

Melo was simultaneously a fairly old-fashioned and extremely modern woman. She was an excellent example of an independent woman who not only worked for her living but also travelled to extraordinary places. She made this appear absolutely normal, and gave me the sense that the world was a place to discover and explore. She often travelled by herself, and made friends and met interesting characters wherever she went. Postcards were dispatched from all the far-flung places she visited. The last postcard I received from her came from Naga Land where she had gone to visit the headhunters. I will never know why my elderly Aunt decided to travel to a remote region of India but I was most proud of her spirit of adventure. She found great joy in investigating new places and meeting new people and even more so in telling the story of her discoveries. An Aunt who went to places other people would find hard to locate on an atlas was a great source of inspiration.

On her last visit to Barcelona where I live, she asked to be taken to the trendiest new restaurant in town. This happened to be a restaurant where you ate in the pitch-dark and where the waiters were all blind. Melo was already composing the story she wished to write and was keen that I translate for her so she could discover who our fellow diners were. As I couldn't even see the other customers, this was an almost impossible task but once again proved the extent of Melo's curiosity about people in general.

For me, my Aunt's writings on her childhood are highly personal glimpses into another era and an evocative portrayal of her life. I hope other readers enjoy them as much as I do.

'Never let the facts get in the way of a good story!'

1. *By the Sea*

Only once when I was a child were we taken for a traditional holiday by the sea. We were back on leave from Ceylon and spent a month with our cousins in a rented wooden bungalow on the cliff above the pier at Rosslare. (Last time I looked, the house was still there, though somewhat nearer the cliff edge.) We brought our ponies and bicycles with us. We should have had a glorious time just like the Famous Five in Enid Blyton's books: roaming the countryside and discovering the secret hidey holes of smugglers, when not swimming out to save people from drowning. As it was, it rained most of the time, icy winds blew damp sand in our faces whenever we went on the beach and the sea was so cold and forbidding that we refused to bathe. The ponies could never be caught and often escaped from their field, so the gangs of diamond thieves and international spies went about their business unhindered while we tried to extract the ponies from the neighbouring gardens unseen.

My happiest memory from that holiday is of being taken

to a fit-up theatre. It was in a long low shed with a stage at one end. The aged green curtains opened in little jumps and starts to reveal the lady who had sold us our tickets as the Gangster's Moll in the opening melodrama and the Virgin Mary in the main production, which was *Our Lady of Fatima*. In this, her face or rather her teeth, because they were her most prominent feature, appeared miraculously through the branches of the painted tree on the back cloth.

Another evening we were brought to the circus. My younger sister Eleanor was about four, and her interest in acrobats and dogs jumping through hoops soon waned. She insisted loudly and clearly that she wished to leave the tent. As she had an undisputed reputation for screaming louder and longer than even a banshee if she did not immediately get what she wanted, the Aunt in charge hastily removed her. They were strolling outside when Eleanor's eye was caught by what might be a new penny that had rolled through some railings. She pushed her head between the bars in order to examine the treasure more closely and found that after all it was only an old beer-bottle cap. Then she found she could not get her head out.

The Aunt pulled and twisted in vain, as did the lion tamer, who had been having a smoke nearby between shows. People collected to give advice – it was proposed that the Strong Man should show off his muscles by wrenching the bars apart, but his wife was very against this as she said 'the back was at him'. One spectator recounted to the enthralled audience how the very same thing had happened to her brother's child and since that time his head wobbled like a tennis ball on a string.

By now Eleanor's plight had become a greater attraction than the circus itself and it was suggested that the priest should be sent for, and the local fire brigade. It was at this moment, the show over, that my brother and I came out of the big top licking ice-cream cones. When we realized that our sister was centre of a large crowd, we were deeply embarrassed and tried to slink away, but she had caught sight of us and her cries, which up till then had had a frightened pathetic note, changed to yells of utter fury; she gave a little flip of the head that released her from the bars, and screeched, why didn't she have an ice cream too, she wanted one NOW!

2. Cork and County Club

Until I was eighteen, my only experience of life in the big smoke was Thursday in Cork – and though there were no doubt parts of Cork where rough and tumble took place, it was not in the Cork and County Club where we would lunch with our uncle and aunt in the ladies' dining room. Though men could enter the ladies' part of the club, no woman was allowed to enter the male precincts in the front of the club. Our door was in a back lane otherwise used for dustbins. The ladies' lobby was panelled in varnished pitch pine with uneven terrazzo tiles on the floor. On the gentlemen's side, it may have been merry jokes and riotous behavior, but it was not like that on the ladies' side. The windows were frosted glass and the dining-room walls decorated with pictures of heaving seascapes. The few scattered couples would acknowledge our presence with a discreet nod and then continue murmuring to each other in low voices over their cutlets.

After she had finished her messages, the Aunt, my brother and I had tea in the ladies' drawing room where we read *Vogue* and

The Sphere in front of a fire. The only lively moment was if one of the members had taken the Aunt's parcels home by mistake.

The Cork and County Club opened in 1829 in a building on the South Mall designed by the Paine brothers. It had originally been The County Club until it united with The Cork Club. They may have regretted this when, at the end of the nineteenth century, a committee member from the city accused another member of cheating at cards – poker, to be precise. The fact that the accuser, Richard Piggot Beamish (owner of the well-known brewery), did not play cards and had not witnessed the game, and that the accused, Joseph Pike, was a longstanding friend and neighbour, did not deter Mr Beamish from reading out the hearsay evidence at a meeting of the committee. Joseph Pike, chairman of the Cork Steamship Company, sued for libel. Beamish pleaded that as senior committee member of the club, he had to conduct an investigation. The jury generously returned a verdict for both plaintiff and defendant. They said the plaintiff did not cheat, but that the defendant did not mean any harm when he accused him of it. Though Pike's reputation remained unblemished, it was perhaps rather odd that his mama should have presented the judge in the case with a handsome residence in Douglas shortly after its conclusion.

A very much more serious event happened on the night of 17 July 1920 when masked raiders pushed passed the doorman and ran into the smoking room, where they fired several shots at Colonel Gerald Smyth, who was sitting down with four other men. He leapt to his feet and got as far as the hallway before dropping dead. Colonel Smyth was a much-decorated officer during the 1914–18 war when he had been six times seriously wounded and lost his left arm while rescuing an injured NCO. Earlier in the year, he had been made the RIC divisional commissioner for Munster and as such, a month before in Listowel, he had made a speech in which he was quoted as having incited the members of the RIC to make reprisals on the local populace. He later denied this, saying he had been misquoted in the *Freeman's Journal*.

Such was the unpopularity of Gerald Smyth that only half the number of jurors needed for the inquest could be persuaded to attend and no engine driver would bring a train with his body back to his home in Banbridge. In Banbridge, after his funeral, there was a furious reaction; £40,000 worth of damage was done to Catholic buildings in the town by rioters and Catholics could not be employed in the factories unless they signed a document to say that they would not support Sinn Féin.

The Cork and County Club closed in 1989 – I never did see the gentlemen's part of the club. Oh, how I wish I had made a stand for women's lib by pushing through the green baize door to see the delights and comforts beyond.

3. Curiosities

Curiosities, as children, we arrived in Ireland from the fabled East, determined to impress our poor little stay-in-the-mud cousins. Vividly, we described Sri Lankan leopards that with one bound sprang through the nursery window and arrived, snarling, at the bottom of the bed to be fended off with pillows. We told of snakes that curled round the branches of the trees under which we walked and how elephants trumpeted at dawn around the bungalow – a bit of an exaggeration.

At last, goaded into desperation for the honour of Ireland, Cousin James said that on the farm there were carnivorous plants and, what's more, if we walked in the Marlow, we could see butterworts with our own eyes. We grew silent and not at all keen to don our wellies for an encounter with a flower hungry for its lunch. Slowly, we followed my uncle down to the boggy field near the river. We were cautious as we climbed over the gate.

I was the first to see an elegant blue flower on the end of a long stalk the size and colour of a large viola. My fears diminished, for who could suspect this beautiful blossom of any malicious purpose? But this was just a delusion, as butterworts proved to be every bit as deadly (though only to very small insects) and rather more fascinating than our apocryphal snakes and leopards. The butterwort plant is a rosette of yellowy-green glistening leaves that exudes a glue to entrap an insect. As the victim struggles, the edges of the leaves curl around to make escape impossible. The prisoner is dissolved by enzymes into digestible components, which are absorbed through the leaf.

The sundew is another species of insectivore that grows on Irish bogs. The spoon-shaped leaves have hair-like tentacles, each of which has a tiny droplet of what looks like dew, hence the name, but is really a sticky corrosive. When an insect is ensnared, the other tentacles bend towards the victim, further trapping it.

At its centre in Lullymore, Rathangan, Co. Kildare, the Irish Peatland Conservation Council has an insect chamber of horrors with the largest carnivorous plant collection in Ireland. Besides the native butterworts, sundews, and the bladderworts that float in water vacuuming up water fleas, there are numerous kinds of showy pitcher plants. An innocent insect, out on the spree, smells delicious nectar, not realizing that it is spiked with narcotics that will cause it to miss its footing and fall to the bottom of a pitcher to drown in the pool of digestive juices. There is also a Canadian pitcher plant that was introduced a hundred years ago to a bog in Longford where it has naturalized. One plant was found to contain the remnants of two hundred and five victims.

Oh, how much safer to be a child in the jungles of the East than to be an insect in the bogs of Ireland.

4. Church in Carrigadrohid

Meadowsweet, willow herb and the dark-purple flowers of deadly nightshade are specks of colour in the rank grass among the graves – brambles stretching long tentacles in from the hedge are seizing the land as their own. The line of ugly evergreen cyprus trees by the gate looks mean and alien. On the far wall the ash and its seedlings are marshalling an invasion force in untidy ranks. I tread cautiously through the clumps of nettles from headstone to headstone, pulling aside the growth that hides the lettering. Ted, beloved husband; Richard DSO, Faithful and True; Eileen, daughter of ... these names were of the people who had gathered for morning service every Sunday. This extension to the graveyard had not been here. I look over the wall and below in the valley on the other side of the road is a BVM – Our Lady – standing in a little sentry box presiding over a garden decorated with stones like a badly mixed cake. It too looks unkempt, the blue paint of her dress flaked away – the plastic flowers that lie at her feet have faded into dull pinks and greens.

On a hill outside a village, two Church of Ireland churches stand near each other. The one on the right has a square tower that was added to the original old church with money from the Fund of the First Fruits in the early part of the nineteenth century. For a long time I thought that this tower had been a cornucopia with bananas, pineapples, cherries and grapes tumbling over the edge of the parapet – and was sadly disappointed when I found out that it is a quotation from St Matthew's Gospel 7:16: 'By their fruits ye shall know them', and the fund was garnered from the income of a clergyman for his first year in a living and applied to the building and repairing of Church of Ireland churches and glebes. Around 1845 an incomprehensible decision was taken to abandon the old church and build a new one across the road. Now the old church stands amongst briars, the roof has long gone and the walls are in danger of collapse but the tower with its pinnacles is still there.

The new church is a small, solid building put up during the Famine, I hope to give employment through those terrible years. There is no tower, only an arch for the bell. Did it toll for the morning service? I can't remember. Who would have pulled the rope? None of the congregation surely, because if so I would certainly have been volunteered. Perhaps the clergyman, but surely he was always hurrying from the service in Macroom. It could not have been the verger, Molly Buckley, for she was attending Mass in the chapel in the middle of the village. In spite of the two churches above the village, the Protestants kept a low profile so perhaps the call to prayer was not sounded over the hills and valleys.

'Oh for a thousand tongues to sing,' we implored the Almighty, for the congregation never exceeded fifteen. Besides my uncle and aunt and me, there was a lady with a brown beret pulled over her ears and a drip on the end of her nose, three colonels and their wives, the colonels having retired to the riverbank to spend the evenings of their lives, rod in hand, while their wives gardened. Then there were the Miss McMullens whose reputation was enhanced in my eyes by their owning a half-rabbit, half-cat – I know it is not possible, but that is what they said it was and that is what it looked like. In the back pew was Commander Wilsden who came to church on a bicycle and from whom we bought eggs; the colonels' wives patronized him because he had been in the navy and was too poor to be interested in fishing. Even in summer there was the smell of mildew, mice and bats in the church. In winter it was intensely cold, the little electric-fire bars hung high up on the walls doing nothing to dispel the clammy chill. The walls were pink, but the paint was flaking off and the mould stains made interesting designs of green and black on the plaster. There were a few dull monuments to departed clergymen of unsurpassed goodness; the windows had no saints or angels in them and the east window was a pattern of intertwining vine leaves with a red border, so that the only pleasure to be had was when the sun, which seemed to shine so seldom when we went to church, shone through either a red or a blue panel and reflected on the face of the clergyman, turning his nose blue or red as the case might be.

My Aunts had very strict ideas about how I should be dressed for church: 'Your good tweed coat and skirt', tight leather gloves in which I had to squash my swollen chilblained fingers, and a hat. The first Christmas I spent there I was given a turquoise velvet beret so I had no need to wear my brown felt school hat. At first I wore socks, white ones that drooped sadly over my sensible shoes and drove Aunt Laura mad so that she bought me nylon stockings and a suspender belt, but the stockings wrinkled round my matchstick-like legs and the seam at the back used to creep about my calves.

The music was supplied by Aunt Laura who played the organ. The colonels would have liked the rousing hymns that they used to hear across the barracks square, but Aunt Laura knew what God liked and God liked traditional Irish tunes better than *Hymns Ancient & Modern*. She took no notice when they begged for more familiar melodies. 'Such nonsense, they don't know one note from another!' she said later over the roast lamb.

To my acute embarrassment and fury, every holiday there was a children's service solely for me as I was the only person under fifty.

5. From Fork to Plate

I am no stranger to locally grown food for when I was young and my parents were abroad, my brother, sister and I spent our holidays with different Aunts and every vegetable that we ate was produced in their various gardens.

The Aunts, though very different in personality, were all knowledgeable and enthusiastic gardeners who had a deep aversion to idle hands when there was work to be done. 'No frowsting indoors on a glorious morning like this!' was the trumpet call over breakfast. We were sent out into the good fresh air where the temperature was only too often sub-zero and the rain lashed down, but any hesitation in putting on our macs and rubber boots was treated with scorn and we would be told that we were not made of sugar and driven forth into the storm.

Toiling in the flower garden was arduous but unexciting – after a single day's work-experience among the eryngium, sweet pea and campanula seedlings, weeding was deemed beyond our meagre intelligence. Raking leaves, pushing wheelbarrows and straightening the edges of the lawn were thought to be more within our capabilities. Occasionally, as a tremendous treat, we were allowed to make a bonfire. The advantage of work in the flower garden was that one could skulk in the potting shed and peruse the seed catalogues or a book, if one had had the forethought to have hidden one there.

Garden-produce Aunts were fiercer and better organized. Peas, beans, apples, gooseberries and strawberries all had to be picked. Not for the dinner table, for alas it was vulgar commerce that had goaded these Aunts to a frenzy of activity. We were only allowed to eat what had been rejected for public sale. 'The birds know best!' said the Uncle as we sank our teeth into apples that had already been tasted by our feathered friends or worse still, strawberries shared with a slug or two, for they were even more discerning and greedier than the birds.

At dawn on Fridays, we were packed into the car with punnets of fruit and baskets of vegetables to sell at the country market. After the first rush of customers and while the Aunt went shopping, we were put in charge of a stall. In the cut and thrust of business, we were but feeble exponents, and in spite of the huge investment in our education, were none too bright about change and easily overawed by the buyers.

Fruit picking is more perilous than one would imagine; I still bear the scars from the thorns of the gooseberry bushes, but it was when picking apples that we diced with real danger. Queenie, a pony of uncertain temperament, resided in the orchard and was likely to attack with bared teeth those she considered invaders of her space. Few can beat my time to the top of a Bramley's Seedling.

The fruit in season went on for a long time or rather, dull old stewed gooseberries, apples and, to a lesser extent, rhubarb, appeared on the menu throughout the year, as one of the summer tasks was bottling these fruit. Bottling involved the likelihood of being scalded by boiling water, searching for the rubber rings that sealed the bottles, which had invariably been mislaid since the year before, and the faint possibility of the kilner jars exploding.

It was my brother who underwent the most painful experience, for once, seeing a ripe plum with an exquisite purple bloom and those in authority not being visible, he plucked it and put it in his mouth; unfortunately a wasp had had the same idea and it stung my brother on the tongue. His yells brought the Aunt to his side, but owing to his tongue swelling up, he was unable to explain what had happened so the Aunt decided he was having a fit and, with vague memories of a first aid course, tried to push a cake of soap between his teeth. When at last he was able to speak through the foam, she was very cross and said it served him right and that he was too old to make such a fuss about a little sting and that the expensive Pears soap was now so mangled it could not be put in the visitors' bathroom: 'It was really too bad.'

In spite of all this fresh home produce, I do not remember our meals being of particular gastronomic delight. There were far too many marrows, like other vegetables boiled thoroughly and often smothered in a lumpy white sauce. Owing to the country market, I often wondered if I had scurvy from lack of vitamin C, though I think I had confused this disease with scurf, more commonly known now as dandruff.

There were also chickens whose eggs had to be preserved in water glass. 'To the Chinese, thousand-year-old eggs are a great delicacy,' we were instructed when we complained of the unpleasant taste of scrambled eggs on a cold winter's morning. 'Just shake on some pepper and salt and they will be delicious.' Most of the Aunts could kill a hen with a single pull and a twist but one Aunt, more sensitive than the others, ordered her husband to do it. He, the most peaceable and unbloodthirsty of men, consulted a friend who said of course she would have done it, but that she was just off to an RSPCA meeting. Then he was told that the postman, who had just left the letters at the house, was an ace executioner. My Uncle ran after the said postman, with the pullet from death row under his arm, but it was not until he had reached the last house in the village that he caught up with him. By this time quite a crowd had collected, interested as to why an elderly gentleman should be running from house to house with a hen under his arm. It turned out that the reputation of the postman hung on the fact that he shot pigeons and he was not at all a hands-on murderer. The spectators offered helpful advice as to its dispatch, which included chopping off its head with a carving knife. This method was rejected as one wit said that it would be difficult to pick out the real headless chicken in the present company.

My Uncle returned with the chicken alive and indignant and we opened a tin of sardines for lunch.

6. *The Confirmation Dress*

I come from a thrifty family and when we lived in Sri Lanka, my mother made all our clothes, though after I was sent back to be educated in Europe the school uniform had to be bought at Dickins & Jones in Regent Street in London. Because I lived in the Irish Republic, to avoid any questions at the border customs post I wore all my new school clothes at once with the result that they were always several sizes too large and my tweed overcoat looked like a dressing gown for my entire school career.

Most of the rest of my wardrobe came from a pool of garments that were handed down through the cousins – it mattered not to our frugal elders that, though closely related, we were not the same shape or height, and this was especially true for the family confirmation dress that had been made for a diminutive, but stout, senior cousin. It came in the post in time for my confirmation, which took place at school when I was fifteen.

I shook the tissue paper from its folds and saw that it was made of limp artificial silk with a skimpy little gathered skirt that was tied round the middle with a stringy sash; pin tucks stretched across my budding bosom. The real horrors were the puff sleeves and the Peter Pan collar. The girls' boarding school I attended was not great at educating us for the halls of academe; rather it saw our future being decided in the ballrooms of large country houses. We knew to a millimetre the width of the hat brim that could be worn at Ascot that year; the correct knot for the scarf that would embellish our outfits when stalking in Scotland and, if not actually riding, how to catch the eye at the Dublin Horse Show. My classmates who were also being confirmed wore crisp white cotton or silk, with ankle-length very full skirts, tiny waists and the scooped necklines that were so fashionable then, and their feet were encased in white court shoes. My legs were like matchsticks and, however much I tightened the suspenders, my nylon stockings wrinkled at my ankles above my sensible Clarks shoes.

I did not realize the full horror of my costume until after I had been confirmed and, with parents and godparents, we were scoffing the festive tea that the school provided. My dress had attended many such functions and though of course it was carefully washed and pressed before every outing, the menus from each could be tracked through the faint marks among the pin tucks, while the spot from the blackberry jam dropped by Cousin Jessica at her confirmation tea the previous September was clearly visible.

None of my friends' brothers came up to chat and indulge in harmless banter over the cucumber sandwiches, no youthful uncle suggested theatre and dinner in the holidays, only the kindly bishop made a beeline towards me, his face beaming with compassion for this child from what he imagined was a financially challenged family. He said: 'Oh, what a pretty dress, my sister had a frock very similar, I remember.' The words were like a knife to my heart and, gripped with an infinite despair, I ate three bowls of strawberries and cream and was just about to start on the fourth when the headmistress caught my eye.

The confirmation dress continued to be sought by my Aunts for their daughters until Cousin Biddy announced that she was not going to be confirmed and locked herself in her bedroom. Her parents and godparents gathered anxiously at the door and though they could only commune through the keyhole, they did eventually elicit that Biddy was not having a crisis of faith, but had burnt the dress in the kitchen boiler.

She did get confirmed – dressed in the tennis frock that was also doing the rounds of the cousins.

7. *L'Aubergine*

I did not pass many exams at school, so, instead of university, I was sent off to learn cooking and dress-making, even though I showed little aptitude for these arts. After a year, I emerged like a butterfly from a chrysalis, as I fondly imagined, ready to be swept off my feet by the strong masterful man with keen blue eyes who was the hero of the many novels I read at the time. Though I fluttered my eyelashes, wore miniskirts and cooked suppers for two in bachelor pads, no gentleman after smacking his lips said, 'Here is the little woman for me.' It may have been because suet pudding was my highest culinary accomplishment.

So I looked further afield and met a Frenchman who was everything one could wish for, including the fact that he spoke more than perfect English. Richard invited me to Paris so that we could go to Longchamps for that illustrious horse race, the Prix de l'Arc de Triomphe.

The occasion demanded looking really smart, but I reasoned frugally that with my dress-making qualifications I could run up a designer outfit from a *Vogue* pattern. I chose a synthetic material, which did not crush but was a little shiny, and plied my needle and thread with fingers that were soon weary and worn, but stitch, stitch, stitch, I completed the garment. This flower of my wardrobe was a maroon trouser suit that I thought both becoming and exceedingly chic, though I never actually saw myself in the whole ensemble, as none of the mirrors at home were full-length so that one had to climb on a chair to see one's lower half.

To say I stunned Richard when I appeared in this costume is to put it mildly. He gave a strangled gasp, turned pale and tottered out to get himself a pair of dark glasses that he wore throughout even though there was no sun. I thought this reception was entirely due to the beauty of my appearance. When we reached the course, I was surprised that Richard was so attentive to my needs; he was always leaving my side to purchase a race card, place my bets, or get me a drink. From my seat in the stand, I could see him having animated conversations with friends, where there were many kissings and shruggings and gestures in a typically French fashion. But when he was with me, he looked straight through anyone who tried to claim acquaintance and pulled his hat further down over his forehead.

He suggested that we should leave immediately after the Arc had been run, but I, determined to quaff the cup of pleasure to the dregs, would have none of it. When we did go, he raced ahead to unlock the car; as I strolled through the carpark, a furious gentleman in a top hat stopped to berate me, and he was soon joined by a chorus of others. Richard, looking as if he was about to rob a bank as his face was now masked in a scarf as well as the dark glasses and the hat, came to my rescue, apologizing servilely to the angry mob. As he hurried me away, he muttered through clenched teeth that my assailants thought I was about to put tickets on their cars. Most unfortunately, much-hated traffic wardens had just been introduced into Paris. They were known as '*aubergines*' because their uniforms, though infinitely better cut and of more expensive material, were of the same colour and design as my trouser suit.

For the rest of the visit Richard arranged for me to attend the great couturier houses to see their autumn collections. I sat on tiny gold chairs and watched open-mouthed as the models strolled down the catwalk in scraps of silver leather and some not very strategically placed feathers. *Vogue* pattern books were a long, long way behind.

8. *St Stephen's Day Walk*

Every year on St Stephen's Day, the slopes of the Cooley Mountains above Ravensdale, north of Dundalk, are dotted with figures climbing up what is known as the Cadger's Pad and then down the other side to Omeath. This walk, the day after Christmas, has become a tradition for the people of Ravensdale and beyond. There is no formal start but at the end most people collect in a hostelry in Omeath. Twenty-eight years ago, Ken Donald and Dermot O'Dowd went across the mountains and back, to work off a surfeit of Christmas pudding. On the next occasion, more people came with them and now about a hundred or so take to the slopes. The Cadger's Pad or path was the way that peddlers or cadgers, as they were called, used to walk with their wares. It is also the way that the Omeath fishermen brought their fish to sell in Dundalk.

As I was brought up on the mountain, I feel possessive about the walk and when I am staying up there, whatever time of year, I like to stroll up the mountain to where, on a clear day, there is a great view of the 'wee county'. Looking down to the left you can see Dundalk Bay and the sea; to the right the Fews Mountains; and straight ahead the town of Dundalk, which is like a grey smudge with what is known as the 'green' church, St Nicolas's Protestant church, with its green copper spire catching the light. These mountains are full of legends of Cúchulainn and his younger self, Setanta, who set out for the king's court at Emain Macha, hitting his *sliotar* before him as he walked. Now there is an annual *poc fada* when twelve competitors hit a *sliotar* on a course around these hills.

In the snow one year when we were children, we brought a heavy wood sledge up to the top of the mountain on the right, which is called Carnavadde, and the three of us got on and pushed off. There was no means of steering it and as we whizzed down my brother and I grasped the fact that we were heading for certain disaster so we abandoned the sledge, leaving our small sister, who had not realized our desertion or the danger, going faster and faster and getting closer and closer to the canyon where the stream runs. Fortunately, the sledge hit a rock before it reached the edge and Eleanor sailed through the air and landed indignantly head first in a snow drift.

At the head of the valley, if you cross over the ridge, directly below is Carlingford Lough and Omeath with the magnificent backdrop of the Mournes sweeping down to the sea. There is no marked path and it is steep, so you have to zig-zag down to the right until reaching the road – I am always glad of my walking poles, which, besides keeping me upright and assisting me over the rocky streams, are useful for prodding boggy patches. Beside the bridge (marked Clermont Pass Bridge on the map) another road leads past Morgan's Fish Factory and down into Omeath and a hot whiskey. Hardier souls than I return over the mountain, but I look round for an acquaintance with whom I can hitch a lift home to cold plum pudding!

9. Cedric

My father was a tea planter so I was brought up on an estate in Sri Lanka where we continued to celebrate our religious festivals as if we were living in Rathgar. On Easter morning, when I was about six, a large silver cardboard egg from my godfather was placed in front of me and when I carefully opened the top, out hopped a tiny, but indignant, bantam cock, which we named Cedric Seebright. He eyed the assembled company malevolently and made a large mess on the linen tablecloth. I was prepared to love and nurture Cedric, and in fact I kept him under my jumper for a short time, but soon, like Macbeth, I was trying to 'cleanse the stuff'd bosom of that perilous stuff'. For such a small bird he had a very sharp beak and razor-like spurs that he used indiscriminately against friend or foe. So Cedric was banished to the backyard to consort with the other chickens.

The hen run was much frequented by me and my brother and my sister, for nothing is nicer, except finding wild mushrooms, than collecting eggs. I still think of it as one of the keenest pleasures in life and as children we eagerly volunteered for the duty. We had little bamboo baskets specially woven for the task. Most of the chickens were Rhode Island Reds, but they were supervised by a fat Australorp with soft iridescent black feathers who looked like a successful Parisian madam. The rooster, a huge white Leghorn, had once been photographed for a Shell petroleum advertisement and since then spent his time practising poses on the hen-house roof.

Cedric revolutionized the hen run – Stalin could have picked up a few tips. The white Leghorn rooster, after a single skirmish, never again strutted with his best side to the camera, but, bald and bedraggled, skulked in dark corners, occasionally joined by the Australorp whose feathers drooped sadly in the mud. The Rhode Island Red hens, on the other hand, thought life was a lot more fun and, squawking excitedly, would run off, not very fast, whenever Cedric cast a cold eye on one of them.

For us, there were no longer any joyous little expeditions to collect eggs. 'Attack, attack,' Cedric would shriek as he half ran, half flew at any man or beast who invaded what he considered to be his territory. To venture into the hen run was now a military manoeuvre. Even when under escort and armed with cudgels, we had to accoutre ourselves in an armour of rubber boots, mackintoshes, and scarves wrapped around neck and face, for Cedric went for the jugular. But as his owner I could not bring myself to sanction Cedric's execution and so it was that he lived to suffer a hero's death.

In Sri Lanka, the great fear always was of rabies. Early one morning the bull terrier belonging to my father's assistant went mad. It bit a dog and two people on the estate and then raced through the yard and in at the open back door of our bungalow to a room where, a few seconds before, my baby sister had been playing on the floor. It rushed on through the house and onto the veranda and into the garden where my father shot it. It was by great good fortune that no one was in its way and that our dog was confined with puppies. The only fatality was Cedric. The mad dog must have run into the yard and Cedric must have gone into his Red Baron mode and launched an attack. All that was left of him was a pathetic little bundle of bloodstained feathers. But for those few vital seconds, Cedric had delayed the dog and probably saved my sister's life.

II

FAMILY

Epistolary Godmother

CHRIS TURNER

Melo, my godmother, once sent me a postcard, a map of the London Underground: 'In case you want to escape,' it read. I kept it for years, a reassuring getaway route from boarding school. She was great at these humorous one-line missives. On a recent postcard addressed to my father, Melo scrawled: 'Come back, come back, my gutters need you —'

Melo, who went to the Hill School in Ceylon (Sri Lanka) with my mother, and later to a secondary school in England called Brondesbury (which, to her amusement, went on to become a training school for Playboy *bunnies), used to visit our family in Belgium. She was a free agent, which impressed me even as a child, and was certainly the most eccentric and bohemian of my parents' friends — she had chickens, apparently too grand to lay eggs, called Edith Sitwell and Sylvia Plath; she ruined a boat-chase scene in the Bond film,* Moonraker, *by shouting to Roger Moore from a Venetian bridge, 'They're behind you!'*

She would borrow a bike and tour the Netherlands for a week or so before returning by train, with 'serious illness in the gears', full of stories of her encounters along the way. Near Arnhem, she wrote in an account of her trip, 'I came out into the grounds of an elegant country house with people strolling along the terraces and sunning themselves in flower-drenched arbours. Everyone was delighted to see me – I thought it was ever such a friendly hotel and tried to book in, but it was the state mental asylum. Mozart and Rasputin both invited me to dine.'

Her generous gifts to me arrived on random dates – never actual birthdays, Jesus's or mine – and were the sort of curios that fascinated a small boy: a brass rubbing she'd made of a knight in armour, a mahogany box filled with an antique geometry set, a book that she worried was too old for me but *'is DEDICATED to you by the author so I hope may be of interest in the future'* (she added that she regularly chauffeured said author around when he summered in Kilkenny and that he *'looks like a gnome'*).

Mainly I learned of Melo, seemingly a long way away in Ireland or other exotic locations (Timbuktu to the Yemen), from her much-anticipated letters, written to my parents and often shared with me. She compiled a well-received book of diary extracts about Ireland, which was fitting because she was an expert chronicler herself. Her epistles, type-written and heavily redacted with XXXXs, always seemed to begin with ingenious, convoluted and glamorous apologies for not having written for so long:

> We had a postal strike for five months and by the time I had discovered a pen, made ink out of elderberries and with a trembling hand started to compose a letter, the pope had descended on Ireland, bringing a halt to all communications except with on High.
>
> I have a lovely excuse. My address book was stolen in Paris. I sincerely hope the robber is a better correspondent than I and that you are receiving lyrical missives in poetical French.

She presented herself as followed by a cloud of woe, which allowed for ample comedy, always self-deprecating rather than self-pitying: *'I wear sackcloth and ashes, I crawl, I rot in hell – my thesaurus goes on for several more pages'* or: *'Even the mice have abandoned ship and gone to build igloos outside'*. Her letters were anything but dull, like those 'appalling photocopied' ones that she dreaded receiving around Christmas:

*The ones that in paragraph 2 list the successes of the horrible children
– and now I have reached the age when para 3 of these letters say
'Bill – Retired in May, but far from stopping work, he finds that he
is busier than ever and has also taken up watercolour/Morris dancing
and is chairman of the local bell-ringing group, while I am still fully
occupied with my Wednesday morning ukulele class.'*

As a university student, I went to stay with Melo in her cottage (of
questionable hygiene) in Lavistown. There were vestiges of a colonial
past – two elephant-feet waste-paper baskets, she explained, were sometimes positioned behind a curtain to create the suggestion of a looming
presence in the room. Melo had taken lodgers and run a B&B there, and
was as expert a hostess as she was a guest. When I missed the weekly
ferry home, after she'd warned me over breakfast that I was cutting it fine,
I rang her, hoping to be invited back. She wasn't having any of it and
dispatched me to a large, empty country house belonging to a deceased
relative. I made a bed among the dust sheets and she joined me a day or
two later to sort through the contents.

Melo was obviously a part of old Ireland. She took me on a tour
of the ancestral Kilkenny Castle, ignoring the velvet ropes as though
showing me her own home. As secretary of the Butler Society, she was
able to locate one of her extended family for me wherever I went in the
world, and they were often part of her own globetrotting tours. The last
time I saw her, she came to stay with me in New York on the way to
visit much more glamorous people – Rockefellers or Morgans – in Cold
Spring Harbor, Long Island. But she was as happy on my airbed as she
was in their four-poster, or so she implied.

Thirty years earlier she'd spent 'two jolly months whizzing around
the States'. Her chief memories were of bus stations, where she cuddled
up to muggers on hard wooden benches. 'Occasionally,' she wrote, 'I was
snatched from this cosy habitat into unknown multi-millionaire homes,
where I was welcomed as a scion of a noble family and expected to
entertain the "m-m'aires".' She gave a lecture in a huge auditorium in
Beverly Hills and had prepared a talk on the Butlers and Kilkenny:

I was shown an invitation which said I was to give a fascinating lecture on silver, glass, pictures and tapestry – It was simply ghastly. I had to give myself a crash course on these subjects and invent practically everything. Fortunately the loudspeaker failed to work and there was absolutely NO time for questions.

She had a luncheon given for her at the Morgan Guarantee Trust in New York, the grandeur of which was offset by having to stay in the YMCA, 'which was actually the local lunatic asylum, a fact that escaped my notice until an elderly lady in a very unrefined pair of velvet shorts came and woofed at me to put a lump of sugar on her nose'.

One got the reassuring impression from Melo's letters that the whole world was mad.

10. *Anaverna*

It is almost a tribal community at Anaverna in County Louth, where Vere Lenox-Conyngham is surrounded not by 'his sisters and his cousins and his aunts', because I, his sister, am not there, but by many of his descendants and also our cousin Kate Okuno who has a house in the yard. His eldest son Edward with his wife Lindis and their three children live in half the house, and in the lodge is his son Thomas, who works for the mural artist Nat Clements.

The pretty enclosed cobbled yard is surrounded by what were the stables, the harness room and the coach house, but they have all undergone a transformation. Kate lives on one side in the converted loose boxes, laundry and apple loft; on the opposite side there are now studios for artists and writers. Siofra O'Donovan worked here on her book *Pema and the Yak*; among other writers to have spent time here are J.J. Harrington and the Afghan poet Dawi Roushaan; painters include Sean Cotter, Samantha McKee and Simon Tarrant; while the Brazilian Raul Araujo worked on

conflict resolution through drama. For several years, the jewel-
ler Mia Mullins had a studio here. Now Nat Clements, who has
worked on Castle Leslie, Lissadel and the TCD dining room, is
using one studio to create the decorations for the newly refur-
bished Ulster Hall, assisted by my nephew Thomas.

In what was a loft above the old coach house, Vere has created
a most attractive concert hall that will seat about seventy people.
The Ensemble Avalon, Syrius Trio and the Korros Ensemble
have all performed here and in July this year [2010], the Carducci
Quartet are returning for a concert and will be holding a
chamber music course. In the foyer, the audience may have wine,
tea or coffee during the interval and there is a room where, in
the winter, there is an open fire so that one can sip one's wine
in comfort. It is very much a family venture: Cousin Kate is the
ticket office, the tea maker and, when I was there last, had to
step into the breach or rather onto the dais when my brother
had a sudden onset of stage fright about making the announce-
ments, before scampering out into the garden to gather a bunch
of flowers to present to the musicians.

My nephew Thomas is called on to cook delicious meals for
the players and my great-nieces are being trained up to present
the bouquets. On a summer evening, everyone is encouraged
to bring a picnic to eat before or after a concert in the old-
fashioned walled garden, with borders bright with flowers – and
weeds. There is a slope of delphiniums that my father planted,
interspaced with scented double narcissi, and between the Irish
yew trees is a croquet lawn. In one corner of the garden is a
summer house built by Kate to replace the original one that was
destroyed fifty years ago when some dynamite, which had been
hidden by unknown people in a shed behind the garden wall,
exploded one night. The housekeeper said, 'God, I never closed
the door of the Aga,' under the impression that the blast had
taken place in the house.

The first owner of Anaverna was Judge McClelland – there is a memorial to him put up by his widow in the church on which is written: 'A humble tribute to departed worth'. In the nineteenth century, the house was let for many years to Sir James Fitzjames Stephen, a Criminal Court judge and uncle of Virginia Woolf (I do not think she ever came here). The judge's passion was trees and their care and it is owing to his attentions that the wood that slopes from the avenue up towards the mountain is still beautiful. Anaverna was bought in 1916 by my grandfather on his retirement from tea planting in Sri Lanka. He was a younger son of the family at Springhill, County Derry, where the Lenox-Conynghams lived for almost three hundred years.

There was no architect employed when the house was put up around 1800. The builder was a local entrepreneur who lived in Ravensdale. His son became a well-known architect in New Orleans – we and the architectural scholars who visit Anaverna from Louisiana like to think that the design of the house was influenced by James Gallagher or, as he called himself in New Orleans, Gallier, but as he was about three years old when it was being built, his assistance can only have been puddling in the plaster!

It is a square house with a wing at the back. There is an elaborate fanlight above the front door and a porch that should not be there as it spoils the symmetry, but theoretically makes the house less draughty. On each side of the door there are two long sash windows and five above. The stucco outside is painted a creamy orange, which sounds garish, but has weathered into the backdrop of trees and the mountain that rises directly behind.

On the long granite steps in front, we would sit in the sun and my mother would bring out tea – she used to make a sponge cake twice a week, though only my father ate a slice and the rest was given to the dogs. They were Pekingese and were the terror of the neighbourhood – particularly of the postman for whom they lay in wait in order to pursue his bicycle down the avenue.

We always forgot to corral the dogs behind locked doors, so they would sneak out to set up the ambush. Then there was the chase with the postman pedalling furiously closely followed by a pack of Pekingeses and lastly by members of the family, with bits of breakfast still adhering to their persons, screaming imprecations. In the end we had to collect our post from the post office.

The most curious feature of the house is a tunnel into the basement. It is not a very long tunnel, and it starts with an open cutting. If a car is left at the back door without putting on the brake, it has vanished when its owner returns. Unless stolen, it is to be found in the deep cutting. The other day, Vere had a difference of opinion with the ride-on mower, which emptied him into the tunnel, but fortunately did not follow him.

The cellars have caves in the outer wall for storing turf, though we said they were dungeons, and certainly with their iron gates with rusty chains that is what they look like. Under the house is the old kitchen, which still has the iron hooks in the ceiling and the old cast-iron cooker. Mrs McNamee, who had been cook here in her youth, used to tell us that it was lovely and warm down there and the staff got up to all sorts of high jinks. But it is hard to imagine these dark, damp, cobwebby rooms being pleasant; the only natural light comes from grills that are set into the grass around the house. When my grandmother came here, she moved the kitchen upstairs.

Lindis has made a kitchen that is very light and modern, though she still has the original Aga that was put in around 1938. She has knocked through a door from the kitchen to what was our dining room and is now a warm, friendly living room. When my grandparents lived here, they ate in the dining room though the food was tepid because it had to be carried along the back passage that led from the kitchen to the far end of the dining room. My parents almost always had meals in the kitchen, but they sat in a chilly little room known as the anteroom. It had three doors and a high ceiling. In theory, it could be warmed up quicker than other rooms with the electric bar balanced in the fireplace – but it was never cosy. When there were guests, my father lit paraffin stoves that gave off a smell, which, when mixed with the aroma of wet dog, used to be synonymous with big houses. A thin, upright oil stove was called 'Old Harry' because, like Uncle Harry, it smoked.

One of the most attractive features of Anaverna are the front stairs that curl up the wall under a big window. The back stairs are in a separate hall and, though utilitarian, they are handsome enough, which makes the division of the house much easier and it also means that Edward and Lindis can expand with their family into the attic.

The fifth generation of Lenox-Conynghams is now playing in the stream that rattles through the wood and has always been a fascination to anyone under ten. They are collecting conkers and staining their hands with green walnuts just as we did when we were their age and the howls still reverberate around Anaverna when they are stung by a bee.

11. *Daphne du Maurier*

I have one thing in common with Daphne du Maurier, the novelist whose centenary is celebrated this year. Not, alas, many of the things I would have liked, but we each have a disreputable ancestor, although her great-great-grandmother was more interesting, beautiful, possibly more wicked, and much more disreputable than my own great-great-uncle.

The du Maurier ancestor was Mary Anne Clarke who is described as having 'dazzling dark eyes that beamed with irresistible archness and captivating intelligence'. She was born in the back streets of London and, after having various lovers, became mistress of George III's second son, the Duke of York – the one who 'led his men to the top of the hill and led them down again'. He installed her in a house in Gloucester Place, which she furnished extravagantly; the solid silver dinner service had belonged to the guillotined royal family of France. She had two carriages, eight horses and numerous retainers. Mary Anne found a handy way of paying for the various items by taking very large sums of money used to influence the Duke of York, who was commander-in-chief of the army, in obtaining commissions, promotions, appointments and exchanges.

Unfortunately, the duke took up with a Mrs Carey, a dancer from Fulham. Mary Anne, in revenge and to get money to pay her debts, disclosed to a Member of Parliament how kind the duke had been to her friends in the army. He brought the information before the House of Commons where a very public enquiry took place; the duke was acquitted 'of personal corruption and connivance at the infamous practices as disclosed by Mrs Clarke', but he had to resign as GOC (General Officer Commanding). It was Mary Anne Clarke who ended up in prison and, when released, went to live in France where her daughter married Daphne du Maurier's great-grandfather.

In my grandfather's house, on the dining-room sideboard, stood a silver tea urn with the inscription that it had been presented in 1810 to Colonel Butler, Commandant of the Royal Military College, by his Royal Highness, the Duke of Clarence. Inside the urn was a letter from Mrs Jordan, a popular actress who had been born near Waterford, and lived for twenty years with the Duke of Clarence (who later became William IV). During their time together she bore him ten children, but continued her acting career. A lampoon of the day asked:

> As Jordan's high and mighty squire
> Her playhouse profits deigns to skim,
> Some folks audaciously enquire:
> If he keeps her or she keeps him.

The recipient of the urn was my great-great-uncle, Colonel James Butler from Priestown, near Mulhuddart in County Meath. As a younger son, he had joined the army and become the lieutenant governor of the Royal Military College at Sandhurst. The letter expresses the gratitude of Mrs Jordan and the duke for the attentions and kindness shown by Colonel Butler to dear George Fitzclarence, their eldest son, when he was at the college.

Sometime later, I am sorry to say, Sandhurst was 'overcome by scandal' when Great-Uncle was accused of tampering with examinations, receiving presents and favouring the sons of the rich and powerful. There was a full enquiry with many witnesses and a coach-load of documents that had to be taken to London. It was established that Uncle James did procure some whiskey through a cadet who came from Scotland, and that he was somewhat vague about why some cadets should be punished lightly for relatively severe offences while others were sent to the Black Hole for some trifling misdemeanour. But the enquiry found Uncle James innocent of the charges of gross peculation and plunder, though he did have to pay for some timber he had sold from the Sandhurst estate. There was no mention of the urn in the enquiry.

George Fitzclarence became a major general. Great-Uncle James retired and died soon afterwards. The urn still stands on the sideboard.

12. *Magic Tap*

I stepped off the Greyhound bus into the warm Texan winter sunshine. Amarillo was then, and perhaps still is, a small town that looked as if it had been dropped like a discarded sweet paper into the desert. Its raison d'être came from the cranes that bowed like obsequious courtiers in the desert directly outside the city. Up and down they dipped, bringing the black gold from the earth.

Oil was the fundamental source of the wealth of my hosts so I hoped for all the reputed flamboyance of Texan millionaires. The house was comfortable and modern, but not particularly ostentatious, though there was a library with a very curious selection of books on the shelves that took me some time to work out. The name of my host was Stanley Marsh. Every title or author included the words either Stanley or Marsh. Therefore there was *Stanley across Africa* next to whodunits by Ngaio Marsh and *The Marsh Arabs* adjacent to the books of Erle Stanley Gardner.

Outside there was little attempt at landscaping the sparse soil, though there was a lake that I would have called a pond, but big enough for an island with a silver tractor. The water tank on its high plinth was painted as a Heinz Baked Beans can and there were some bored peacocks. But beyond the scrubby fir trees, far out into the desert, there blossomed not prize cacti but a row of Cadillacs. There were ten of them with their noses buried deep in the sand and their tail fins pointing at an eighty-degree angle towards the sky. It was bizarre, but it was also spectacular, both an art form and a folly.

In Ireland there is any amount of garden ornamentation and follies. Most were built at the end of the eighteenth century and include *cottages ornés*, grottoes and towers. Only the other day I saw a new architecturally designed house perched among the branches of a tree. My father, always keen to embellish his garden, craved statues that he found he could buy very cheaply in a garden centre, but as they were made of plastic with a seam down the sides my mother forbade them. So he ended up with the magic tap.

It was not beautiful but it was interesting, being a tap in the middle of the lawn with no apparent connections so that it looked as if it was floating about three feet from the ground. A continuous gush of water poured from the spout into a basin below. It had none of the elegance of the eighteenth-century follies nor the flamboyance of the Cadillacs but, for many of the visitors who came to see the garden, it was more beguiling than strolling among the roses and herbaceous borders.

One afternoon, a guest sneaked back to examine the tap in detail to find out how it worked. As he was inspecting it, he heard cries for help and going to the front of the house found that a girl who had been cleaning the upstairs windows had fallen out onto the granite steps twenty feet below. She was badly hurt and was rushed to hospital, but survived and recovered all the use of her limbs. If it had not been for the attractions of the magic tap, she might have lain on the front steps for hours for we always used the back rather than the front of the house. So, as my father put it rather smugly, it can be wise to have a folly.

13. *Phoenix Park*

Almost my earliest memory is that of my parents having a bitter row in the zoo as to whether my sister, aged two, should be allowed to visit the lion house. 'The smell alone would poison one so young,' my father yelled at my mother. 'She would be traumatized for life by the sight of those beasts.' My mother told him that no child of hers was made of milk and water. Meanwhile, I could see that dear little Eleanor had crawled, unaccompanied, through the doors into the lions' den. Secretly I hoped that a lion would find her a tasty morsel as she was a real pain as a sibling.

Dublin Zoo is situated in Phoenix Park, that great public space that was created by the first Duke of Ormonde. The land had belonged to the Knights Hospitaller until the dissolution of the monasteries when it became crown property. During his time as Lord Lieutenant of Ireland for the second time in 1663, the Duke of Ormonde conceived the idea of turning it into a park. His motives were not entirely altruistic as he had found Dublin

Castle in a miserable state of repair and almost uninhabitable; so he prevailed upon the king to enlarge the park by another 450 acres by buying up the Chapelizod estate and fitting up the house as an official summer residence for the Lords Lieutenant.

He met with opposition from the king's mistress, Barbara Villiers, Lady Castlemaine, who had already received a grant for the place from the king and was furious when it was cancelled. At Ormonde's next visit to court she 'fell upon him with a torrent of abusive language with all the rancour that her heart could suggest and told him that she hoped to live to see him hanged'. The duke replied that he was not in so much haste to put an end to her days, for all he wished was that he might live to see her old!

It was not until the 1770s that it became a people's park when the gates were opened wide to 'tag, rag and bobtail'. And, horror of horrors, the Sabbath was abused by allowing hurling matches to be played on Sunday evenings.

The Duke of Ormonde was born James Butler on 19 October 1610. It was the beginning of a century when Ireland was turned from a country dominated by great feudal dynasties to a Protestant central colonial government. David Edwards, in his book, *The Ormond Lordship in County Kilkenny 1515–1642*, describes how the duke more or less abandoned the feudal allegiances of the previous earls. The Bishop of Ferns said that Ormonde was a 'great bramble, cruelly scratching and tormenting Ireland'. But four hundred years later we can still admire the transformation that he initiated in Dublin. The city expanded and he encouraged the broad straight streets and leafy public squares. Ormonde Quay was constructed with buildings facing the river so that the Liffey became an important visual feature rather than hidden behind high warehouses and sheds; public buildings were 'raised for beauty as well as use', the most important of which was the Royal Hospital.

James Butler was the great-great-nephew of Black Tom, tenth Earl of Ormond, who had fought the last pitched battle between private armies in the British Isles. James Butler remembered the earl when he was old and blind but would 'cherish him in his arms'.

As his father had been drowned in the Skerries, the boy was made a ward of the king and put in the indifferent care of the Archbishop of Canterbury where he had very little schooling and was not fed or clothed properly. When he grew up he had himself taught Latin and Irish. After he inherited the Ormond earldom, he was made Lord Lieutenant of Ireland by the ill-fated Charles I, but after surrendering Dublin to the parliamentarians, he went into exile in France with the future Charles II who made him a duke.

At the Restoration, he was again made Lord Lieutenant and on his landing in Dublin Bay, the Catholic peasantry, who had been badly treated by the Cromwellians, came out to welcome him on the beach, singing '*Thugamar Féin an Samhra Linn*' ('We Brought the Summer In') while they strewed his path with flowers. In spite of being the king's man in his affiliations, he fell from favour at court – the mistresses of Charles II had great political influence and it was suggested that he was no ladies' man. Several of the king's favourites were determined to undermine him. The duke said, 'Nothing of this shall ever break my heart, for however it may fare with me at court, I am resolved well in the Chronicle.' Among his enemies was Captain Blood, who at the Restoration had not received back his estate in Ireland. He plotted to kidnap Ormonde, attack Dublin Castle and lead a general rising in the country; however, his plans were betrayed by informers and Blood met with strong opposition, but escaped.

A few years later, he snatched the duke from his carriage in St James's in London, tied him up and put him on a horse with his son. They rode off to Tyburn where Ormonde was to be hanged, but as Blood adjusted the noose, Ormonde escaped. Blood's next escapade was to attempt to steal the crown jewels. He flattened the crown to put it under his coat, stuffed the orb down his trousers and filed the sceptre in two, but he and his accomplices were caught on their way out. Inexplicably, the king pardoned Blood and gave him back his lands in Ireland.

The duke was ousted as Lord Lieutenant, until Charles II said crossly: 'Yonder comes Ormonde; I have done all I can to make him as discontented as the others, but he will remain loyal in spite of my teeth; I must even take him in again as he is the fittest person to govern Ireland.'

The duke died at his house in Dorset. In order to take his body to London, it was rolled in a waxed winding sheet and put into a lead coffin that was encased in a thick wooden coffin. This was filled with pitch and wrapped in velvet and taken in a hearse attended by six mourning coaches. He was buried in Westminster Abbey on Saturday night, 4 August 1688.

14. *The Mink Coat*

Inheriting a mink coat is no easy legacy nowadays. Not only is fur so politically incorrect that there is a danger of receiving unflattering comments or even having missiles hurled in one's direction, but there is also the difficulty of finding places to wear it. My sister, who inherited the coat, is now eager to attend any elegant outdoor event and can be seen roasting in marquees up and down the country. She was once mistaken for a grizzly bear when peering through the dahlias at an autumn garden party. Our aunt, who was the original owner of the mink coat, made a great fuss every spring about putting it into cold storage in Barnardos, who have been furriers in Dublin for almost two hundred years; their shop in Grafton Street is still run by the family. They are now the oldest manufacturing furriers in Europe.

John Barnardo came to Ireland from Germany in 1823 and started the business in Dame Street. He married Abigail O'Brien as his second wife, and his ninth child, Thomas, was born in 1845 and educated at St Patrick's Cathedral Grammar School.

He remembered the master as being 'the most cruel and most mendacious I have ever seen'. Not considered academic, Thomas Barnardo was apprenticed to a wine merchant. But he abandoned this employment after he joined the Plymouth Brethren, a sect that had originated in Dublin during the Protestant religious revival that swept through Ireland in the nineteenth century. He volunteered for the Chinese inland missions and in preparation went to London to study medicine.

Throughout his studies he continued his evangelical work – not always successfully. Once, when he was preaching in the street, he had a pail of slops poured over him from an upstairs window and another time a lump of mud went straight into his open mouth, stopping him in full flow. He was teaching in a ragged school, when one night a small boy pleaded to be let stay by the fire, as he had no home. Barnardo made the boy take him to the 'lay' where he usually slept. There he found eleven boys clad in rags, huddled together for warmth, on top of a roof with a few wisps of straw but no shelter from the sharp and biting wind. Shocked, Barnardo rented a house as a refuge for thirty-three boys. The number of children was limited until an eleven-year-old boy who had been denied admission pending a vacancy was found dead in an empty barrel. Immediately, Barnardo made a rule that no destitute child would ever be refused admission, and from then on the homes expanded rapidly. On his marriage, a well-wisher gave him and his wife a house, part of which was used as a home for girls. It was here he built his first children's village where cottages accommodated ten girls with a housemother.

By this time Barnardo had given up all idea of going to China and had also stopped attending medical school (he eventually took his degree in Edinburgh after being accused of calling himself 'Doctor' under false pretences). He had an incredible capacity for hard work and was forever implementing new projects, which, he said, came to him in dreams; but he would allow no one but himself to be in charge and it was only after a painful court case that he reluctantly accepted trustees and a committee for his homes.

Thomas Barnardo was a small man, five-feet-three-inches tall, with very poor sight; as he grew older he had to use an ear trumpet. He was always dapper and had his cuffs specially made to button on to his shirt, carrying a spare pair so he could change them if needs be. As a parent he expected his children to follow his strict evangelical discipline, though later his eldest daughter married Henry Wellcome, the American founder of Burroughs Wellcome. After their divorce, she briefly married the writer W. Somerset Maugham. She then became an influential interior decorator, introducing the 'all-white drawing room' to fashionable London.

Financing Barnardo's homes was a perpetual anxiety, but he determined never to turn a child away. When he died the homes were found to have debts of £249,000 – in spite of his imaginative ideas for fundraising. Once he hired the Albert Hall to show the activities of the homes in a series of tableaux. Blacksmiths, printers, wheelwrights, tinsmiths, cooks, tailors and bakers all at work filled the stage and then a few minutes later the space was filled with babies, cots, tea-tables, rocking horses and even a miniature hayfield to show the environment for the youngest children. A game of cricket was demonstrated by disabled boys – Barnardo said to have kept them away would have been to admit they were inferior to other children.

His first donation had come from a servant girl who heard him describing the poor children in London and handed over her savings, a little parcel of twenty-seven farthings. He sought money from both the rich and poor. He held the first street collection in London and had fundraising open days, founders' days and birthday parties in the homes. He solicited contributions through the two magazines he edited and he formed the Young

Helpers' League, with eleven thousand members, for the children of the well-to-do to extend practical help and support. During his lifetime, he received about £3 million in aid of his work.

Thomas Barnardo died at the age of sixty on 9 September 1905, one hundred years ago today. Sixty thousand children had passed through his homes – children whom society had ignored and allowed to subsist in utter misery and degradation on the streets until they were found by Dr Barnardo.

15. *The Damask Tablecloth*

In my family, there is a miniature of an eighteenth-century lady with a turned-up nose that is passed down from eldest daughter to eldest daughter. With the miniature, alas, I have also inherited the nose, which is not an endearing button beloved by romantic novelists but a proboscis that one could hang a hat on, as one of the in-laws unkindly remarked.

There are no emerald tiaras or diamond necklaces amongst our other family heirlooms, though at one time there was a brooch that, in a will dated 1873, was described as 'set with two of my grandmother's teeth which only fell out at the age of eighty-seven years' but fortunately it has either disappeared or is treasured by some other branch of the family. We are not sure if the lion's claw set in gold should be an heirloom or not, for no one is certain if it is the claw of the lion that ate Cousin George in Zululand at the beginning of the century and we don't like to revere just any old lion's claw. But our most venerated possessions are a white damask tablecloth and twelve napkins, all much stained, which came to us in the following way:

My great-great-grandfather was a humble curate in the cathedral town of Lichfield in Staffordshire. He was in love with the archdeacon's daughter, but her family considered that he was her equal neither in birth nor fortune and bitterly opposed the match. Also in Lichfield lived an elderly lady, Miss Lucy Porter, the step-daughter of Dr Johnson, the author of the dictionary. She was very fond of Great-great-grandpapa, though once when she was opposed in conversation by him she said, 'Why, Mr Pearson, you are just like Dr Johnson, I think. I do not mean that you are a man of the greatest capacity in all the world like Dr Johnson, but that you contradict every word one speaks, just like him.'

She also used to tell him that on her death he would not be forgotten, which he took to mean some little keepsake, but when the will was read it was found that she had left him a house, a great deal of money and a number of relics of Dr Johnson. These included the manuscript of the dictionary, a bust of Dr Johnson taken after his death, his walking stick and an enormous table-cloth with twelve huge napkins.

Now that my great-great-grandfather had inherited a fortune, the archdeacon had to withdraw his opposition to the marriage of his daughter though the bride's mother was so annoyed about the nuptials, she stayed in bed all their wedding day.

The couple lived happily ever after, though I am ashamed to say they did not take the care of the Johnson mementoes that they should have. My great-great-grandmother said Dr Johnson was 'a gross old man and a dirty feeder' and she tossed the things up into a loft. Some time later an American came and offered a thousand pounds for the manuscript copy of the dictionary, which caused her to scurry off to look for it, but alas the rats had already found and gnawed through most of it. The bust of Johnson was put on a shelf from which it fell and was shattered into little pieces when someone slammed the door in a huff. The walking stick was burnt in a house fire, so only the tablecloth and napkins remain.

Nowadays the stains are the most interesting part of the tablecloth. Is this where the Great Cham of Literature slopped his chocolate when he topped it up with cream or melted butter? Is that the mark of a leg of pork, boiled till it dropped off the bone? The very dark stain is probably the outside cut of a salt buttock of beef or is it where the veal pie with plums and sugar was spilt? For all of those were Johnson's favourite dishes and they say you can tell a man by what he eats.

16. *Funerals*

My mother disliked the pomp and circumstance of funerals. She wanted a simple burial, with a horse and cart rather than a hearse. When she died, however, horses and carts were no longer in common use, so we tried to obey her wishes in other ways. We had a hearse and undertakers, who are always suitably dressed for the occasion and far more sombre than the relations. A church trolley lurked in the background, so the coffin could be trundled down the aisle like the in-flight food on an aircraft. We chose the plainest possible coffin, forsaking varnish and figured sides. We refused a 'corpse-covering veil' – a euphemism for a shroud – and eschewed the advertised embalming, which promised Mother would 'appear to us in as close to a lifelike appearance as possible and make our last memory pleasant'. But when we received the substantial bill, we found that we had failed to cancel the swansdown lining.

When my father died, two years later, we were determined not to employ an undertaker. Our clergyman was supportive, and he advised against the use of handles on the coffin, as they are only there for show. I thought of Lady Bellew, who many years ago in Kilkenny took evening classes in woodwork. While other students were there to build utilitarian things such as bookshelves and pipe stands, Lady Bellew went just to build her own coffin. We were not that industrious, but someone in the business owed us a favour; otherwise it would have been difficult to find a reasonably priced coffin, as some undertakers seem to operate a closed shop with coffin makers. Our coffin came without screws. My brother considered them too ornate. Consequently, there was much searching at the back of the garage and in the cupboard in the greenhouse, where one of us had saved some long screws. Perhaps it was my father's spirit that guided us to the famille rose snuff jar in the dining room.

We laid out my father in the coffin. It was not really my father but a frail body with skin like paper, his elegant hands seeming more like claws, his eyes, once so very blue, now closed and the nose more sharply prominent than it was in life. Would he have thought it *lèse-majesté* to be eased into his coffin by his children? He would certainly have preferred us to a stranger. But it would have annoyed him to be unable to give directions on how we could have done it better.

We chose the hymns and, with the help of the rector, printed the order of service. The verger's husband dug the grave – which has to be almost two metres deep – and my brother went to an upholsterer for webbing to lower the coffin with. Luckily, he spotted just in time that they were about to give him elasticized webbing, and changed it to the standard kind.

The coffin lay on two chairs in the drawing room until the next evening. In this interregnum, friends came with condolences and sympathy, with cakes and with biscuits for the open house after the funeral.

The brother-in-law's Volvo, on duty as a hearse, took the coffin to the church, which looks over Dundalk Bay from the shadow of the Cooley Mountains. St Mary's is an ancient, plain building, cruciform with a tower at the west end. Its exterior has pale plaster that makes it seem like a lighthouse in the landscape. The bell tolled as we came through the gates. It is known as the hurry-up bell, and we had often scuttled up the aisle after my father, who hated being late. We picked flowers from the garden where my father had laboured alone for the past twenty years, growing vegetables and soft fruit and creating a dramatic slope of blue delphiniums, irises and white, scented double narcissi, as well as the more ordinary herbaceous borders. Our wreaths surrounded the coffin, which rested on trestles rather than what is known as a reposal table.

At the funeral we sang his favourite hymns: 'Oh God, Our Help in Ages Past'; 'Praise, My Soul, The King of Heaven'; and 'Be Thou My Vision', a hymn that has been translated from Irish and is sung to a tune of folk origin called 'Slane'. From the door of the church we could see the Hill of Slane, where in 433 AD St Patrick had lit the first paschal fire, to celebrate the triumph of Christianity over paganism. A grandchild read the lesson from the fifteenth chapter of Corinthians: 'O death, where is thy sting? O grave, where is thy victory?' At the end of the service the coffin was carried out by his descendants, nephews and a neighbour plucked from the congregation. My relations were taller than the neighbour, who had to hold his hands over his head like a caryatid, but my father was not a heavy man, and they negotiated the short walk to the family plot through the graveyard of tombs surrounded by iron railings, headstones and mausoleums.

The coffin was lowered into the grave, with some trepidation about the strength of the webbing. A board was placed over the opening, onto which we laid the flowers we had carried from the church. The clergyman intoned: 'Earth to earth, ashes to ashes, dust to dust; in sure and certain hope of the resurrection to eternal life …'

After the crowd departed two neighbours filled in the grave. Later we returned to tidy it up. It would be a few months before the ground had settled enough to put up the carved slate head-stone. When it arrived we dug a narrow, wide hole, about sixty centimetres deep, and put bricks at the bottom, as a founda-tion, before positioning the stone. My father would have been pleased with the artistry of the mason's calligraphy. He would, I know, have preferred this more permanent memorial to a con-ventional funeral.

III

LOCAL HISTORY

The Rally, Post-Melo

JAMES DELANEY

The 2012 Butler Rally will, I am sure, be as enjoyable as all our other rallies have been. But for many it will also be a sad gathering as the first rally 'post-Melo'. Her welcoming smile and air of being in absolute control of every eventuality must have been reassuring for many 'first-timers'. I think she always came to the opening of the rally with a kind of relief that all the catastrophes she had envisaged had not (yet) happened; however, as the numbers grew and the buzz of conversation and laughter swelled, Melo would withdraw into herself and observe with a quiet satisfaction that seemed to make all the hectic worry of the lead-up worthwhile. We who knew her over a long number of years will remember her like this. We will also remember her as the person who could find seats for members who had forgotten to book for the bus trips – there were always cars to be requisitioned if need be.

Melo could renew flagging enthusiasm with promises of good coffee and lovely scones, not to mention the possibility of – maybe – meeting some celebrity, pop star or actor. But Melo could be awe-inspiring, too, and I have seen a flash in her eye quell incipient revolution when some

Butlers were foolhardy enough to complain that their shoes were not suitable for trudging up an avenue that the bus driver refused to negotiate. 'What were they thinking of not to wear sensible shoes!'

Then again I remember an outing where there was a lot to see and not much time to spare. Some were rash enough to ignore Melo's cry of 'Back to the bus' and lingered to decipher a tombstone inscription, but Melo was having none of that and firmly announced that there was a schedule to be kept and the bus was leaving. This resulted in one lady getting stuck in the narrow gate and we were treated to the sight — and sound — of her being pulled by her husband and pushed by two friends while Melo walked serenely to the bus, where she later greeted them with a welcoming smile when, puffing and panting, they climbed aboard ready for the next adventure.

Melo was a gracious hostess who made unforgettable meringues that were second to none. This reminds me of the story of the famous Russian ballerina Anna Pavlova who was especially fond of a combination of meringue with raspberries and cream, now to be found on menus all over the world as 'Pavlova'. After her death in 1931, a memorial performance of Swan Lake with her old troupe was arranged but with no ballerina in the role she had made her own. Instead, a spotlight played on the stage, following what would have been her movements in the role of the swan. It is said to have been one of the most moving performances ever given.

At this year's rally, I feel that Melo's presence will be everywhere until one almost expects to come face to face with her round the next corner. She will be much talked about and there will be many a smile and only the odd tear. I think she would have wanted it to be like that. She was not the crying type.

17. Rallying the Clans

'I have lost two buses bursting with Butlers,' I wailed as I scanned the empty Tipperary horizon from the Rock of Cashel. The look of surprise on the faces around me made me explain that it was the Butler family, not the useful butlers that hand round bottles of port. Happily we were soon reunited as they had been taken on a short detour to look at a nearby ruined tower house that had belonged to their ancestors.

The Butlers are one of the great Norman families with an illustrious history in Ireland. Every three years they hold a rally based at their ancient stronghold of Kilkenny and for a week there is a programme of lectures, visits to the houses and castles connected with the Butlers, dancing and, appropriately for the Butlers, lots of eating and drinking in Kilkenny Castle.

We had visited a high cross and been entertained by the owners of the nearby Georgian house that was decorated with notices in wobbly lettering announcing: 'Mother, father, grand-mother and CHILDREN cleaned up this house for the Butlers'.

The tiny workers greeted us excitedly with plates of biscuits, cakes and coffee. We lunched at Lisnavagh, a Victorian granite pile where we were welcomed by Lord and Lady Rathdonnell, a niece of one of the founders of the Butler Society. This event is a fixture of the rally and many of the Butlers have been here so often before that they are like old friends, who are able to show off the garden and to point the way to the antique loos flushed by chains and the walls decorated with Spy cartoons. When a tap broke, the hero of the hour was John Butler, a plumber from the north of England. With the diversity of members, we are able to call on expert help in most emergencies.

The first Butler Rally was in 1967, and was attended by over four hundred Butlers from as far afield as Stockholm and Bogotá and it was here that the thirtieth Chief Butler, the Marquess of Ormonde, announced that he was giving Kilkenny Castle, the family home for six hundred years, to the city of Kilkenny. Now it is open to the public and of course to the Butlers on their triennial rallies.

The Butlers were not the first to hold a family get-together: the O'Malleys have fifty-three annual gatherings behind them, while in 1963 the O'Mahonys received embossed invitations, in the name of their chief, Vicomte de O'Mahony, to gather and dance in Dunmanus Castle. They came in their hundreds from all over the world and the Vicomte welcomed them in French, standing on the rocky shore among the clumps of golden gorse and drifts of bog asphodel. He explained that the ruined castle did not belong to him, nor was it suitable for a ball, and, furthermore, he had not known about the invitations; they had been sent out by the enthusiastic genealogist, Eoin ('the Pope') O'Mahony, who stood beaming and unapologetic by his side. The rally was a wild success for 'the Pope' imbued the occasion with his special magic and charisma. The only man who complained was a journalist who had brought a suitcase containing his white tie and tails.

From that time many different families have had gatherings: Egans, Cassidys, O'Conors, Brennans, O'Garas, Foxes, to name but a few. They vary in length from a day to a week, but most of them are held over a weekend. One may wonder at the reasons for these rallies, which are organized by dedicated members of the various clans, who have to work very hard for no remuneration. But as Hubert Butler wrote, 'They bring together the scattered branches and for a few days ties of blood and family count more than the national and political differences which inevitably divide us and, importantly, they preserve the records, the history and the still living traditions.'

Many of the clans have journals or have encouraged writers of genealogy to write down their family history. On their websites one can find a variety of legends that have been commemorated in different ways. The McShanes, for instance, have a rampant lion grasping a bleeding shamrock on their shield and their war cry is 'Anticipate', which I should think would make any enemy quake in their boots. The Doyles have a tartan, with the colours 'green for the Irish; red for the warlike Danes; and Gold for Glory and Wealth' to symbolize their history.

The programmes for the various rallies vary considerably; some have a genealogical emphasis; most of them tour sites of interest to the family. The Sheridans at their rally had a re-enactment of the destruction of Granard by Edward Bruce when, dramatically, a church made of cardboard and straw was set ablaze. During the actual battle in 1315, many of the Sheridans were burnt to death inside the church but in the interests of future rallies, they were spared on this later occasion.

In July, the Lawlors/Lalors are having Gaelic games for all ages in Abbeyleix. At their last rally, their hurling team was victorious over the Ballypickas, perhaps because the referee was a Lalor! I once attended a hurling match when the Brennans, at their gathering, took on the rest of the world, which was certainly more spirited than anything attempted at the Butler rallies. The Crowleys are playing the ancient sport of road bowling during their rally in Bantry this September, which sounds good fun, though it will be hard to beat the McDermotts with the wedding of the daughter of The Mac Dermot, Prince of Coolavin, held in Markree Castle (the Butlers can boast that their rallies have been the cause of two marriages and one divorce).

This year, the Kavanaghs are having their rally immediately after a historical conference on their original territories, Hy Kinsella. During the rally there will be a ceremony in the ancient ecclesiastical centre of St Mullins when the white wand of power will be passed from the present chief, Celia Kavanagh Boylan (when she is not undertaking her role as chief, she is estimating the daily requirement of bread for Merseyside and North Wales), to the new chief from California, Dr Gary Cavanaugh. They will hold their banquet in Borris, the beautiful country house incorporating the original castle, owned by Andrew Kavanagh, a direct descendant of the McMorrough Kavanaghs, kings of Leinster.

The Irish diaspora has extended to every corner of the world, but the Internet has done much to help spread the word of these family reunions. 'With the Internet they are a joy to organize,' Dr Flannery of the Flannery Clan told me. Even administrative officers of the clan do not have to be in Ireland. The chief herald to the Kavanaghs, colourful and energetic Jim Cavanaugh, who instigated the first Kavanagh rally and has done much of the organization for the rally to be held in September, lives in his eco resort in Belize.

Rallies bring back members of the clans from the most distant corners of the world – the Butlers had fifteen different nationalities at their last rally – and the participants are from every walk of life, though I am not sure if the train robber Isaac Flannery, who appears in the Flannery Hall of Fame between a boxer and an astrophysicist, has actually attended one of the Flannery rallies.

At Bantry in West Cork this September, a Crowley knight in full armour, who is flying in from California for the occasion, will protect the Crowleys from any passing foe. Though I doubt if he will have to unsheathe his sword for there is always a Céad Míle Fáilte, the traditional hundred thousand welcomes, for all who come to a rally. The Longford Pipe Band will pipe the Farrells into town and there will be much singing, music and dancing, as at all the rallies. It is an opportunity to trace back the family tree, to visit places that would not be seen by the casual tourist and to meet the Irish relations. As we say over here, there will be great craic.

18. *Kathleen Mavourneen*

Long ago I fell in love with a tenor. Alas, I am not musical so was unable to be his accompanist — he had to do it himself, while I leant against the piano gazing adoringly down his larynx. Oh, how my heart melted as he sang:

I'll wait for the wild rose that is waiting for me,
Where the mountains o' Mourne sweep down to the sea.

Tears filled my eyes when he ended his solo performance with 'Kathleen Mavourneen':

Oh, hast thou forgotten soon we must part?
It may be for years, and it may be forever.

And so it proved to be — as that very day, he went out of my life and into the waiting arms of a soprano.

Whenever I hear John McCormack singing, 'Then why art thou silent, thou voice of my heart?' I feel a twinge of pain for the past.

The composer of 'Kathleen Mavourneen', though so sorrowful at leaving Erin, never actually visited Ireland. Frederick Crouch was born two hundred years ago this July, into a family of musicians in London. By the time he was nine, he was wielding a bow as a cellist in an orchestra when not singing in the choirs of St Paul's and Westminster Abbey. Perhaps this was too much for him for he ran away to sea, but life as a sailor proved to be not what he hoped. Back in London he studied at the Royal Academy of Music and played in Queen Adelaide's private band. However, he never could stick at anything for long so became a travelling salesman in Plymouth. He married there and had sixteen children whom he abandoned, and left with another lady for America.

The second daughter of the marriage was Elizabeth Emma, who had red hair and large dark eyes that she used to great effect when she was living in Paris. As Cora Pearl, she became a legendary *demi-mondaine* of the Second Empire. She attracted many wealthy admirers, including the nephew of Napoleon, who supported her lavish lifestyle. A certain frisson was added to one of her entertainments for, besides the special dish created by Escoffier and named after her, she bathed in champagne in front of her guests, while another time she danced a cancan on a carpet of priceless orchids. At one supper party, she was carried in on an enormous platter, naked except for a sprinkling of parsley.

Her father, Frederick Crouch, meanwhile, was endeavouring to earn a living in the States, teaching singing and giving concerts. In the Civil War, he joined the confederate army as a trumpeter. He survived the war to become a varnisher in a factory in Philadelphia and died in 1896.

There were at least two silent films made of 'Kathleen Mavourneen'. The plot of this melodrama has a wicked landlord falling in love with a comely maiden seen dancing at the crossroads. He insists that her family will be evicted unless she marries him, which in a dream she does; then the wicked landlord regrets the marriage and plans her murder but she is rescued by her true love. True Love, who kills a man during the rescue, is hanged for murder. Kathleen is woken from her dream by True Love; the wicked landlord withdraws his threat and everyone lives happily ever after.

The 1919 silent film starred Theda Bara, the original vamp of the silver screen. Her popularity was based on such films as *Sin*, *The Serpent* and *The Tiger Woman* in which she appeared with her eyes heavily kohled and wearing more barbaric jewellery than clothes. There were indignant objections from two American-based societies, the Central Council of Irish Associations and the Friends of Irish Freedom, that the innocent young Irish colleen was being played by an American Jewess from the Midwest who was not even in her first youth. The film was an expensive flop.

Mavourneen, mavourneen, my sad tears are falling.

19. *Walter Butler: Traitor or Hero?*

For an hour in the cold, cold February morning, I stood in the queue that slowly wound between the underground station and the Wallenstein Riding School attached to his palace in Prague. Czechs of all ages and shapes stood in the queue uncomplainingly and philosophically, allowing me to get a cup of coffee with which to warm my numbed hands. We were queuing to see the exhibition on Albrecht von Wallenstein that had already been running for three months and was to be extended by another two weeks because of its popularity. Wallenstein had been the most successful general to fight for the Holy Roman Empire during the devastating Thirty Years War and I was in the Czech Republic to give a talk on his assassination by an Irishman.

In Prague in 1618, the Protestant citizens had tossed their Catholic governors out of the window of the castle. The governors had survived, which some attribute to a miracle and others to the dung heap that broke their fall, but this incident began the Thirty Years War. Though the Protestants were soon defeated and driven out of Bohemia, the war raged on, involving countries as far apart as Sweden and Spain, and caused the death of half the population of Central Europe.

Wallenstein, a Czech, was first of all a businessman who struck extremely lucrative deals for his services to the emperor; he was a brilliant administrator, running his enormous estates and his armies with remarkable efficiency and he was also a victorious general. But his power and ambition frightened the emperor who dismissed him once, then after a series of defeats had to recall him. Wallenstein was suspected of conspiring with the enemy and was about to be sacked a second time when he was assassinated on the initiative of Colonel Walter Butler, an Irish mercenary who was certain that Wallenstein was planning to go over to the enemy.

In the eighteenth century, Friedrich Schiller, the German playwright, wrote a play on the murder of Wallenstein in which he describes Butler as having been a stable boy in Ireland with a hankering for titles, but Walter Butler, whose family came from a castle in Paulstown, County Kilkenny, was the great-great-grandson of the third Earl of Ormond and had no need for handles to his name. He had come from Ireland to fight for the Holy Roman Emperor with a regiment of Irish Dragoons. Luckily he had a much more appreciative biographer than Schiller in a Father Carew who described him as 'My most esteemed Butler with whom I had lived, passing a most delightful time.' Father Carew came from Tipperary and became chaplain general to all the English, Scottish and Irish forces of the Holy Roman Emperor.

In the winter of 1634, Butler was guarding the passes against the enemy when he received orders from his generalissimo, Wallenstein, to march with him towards Prague. Butler was immediately suspicious for this would leave the way open for the enemy. With his fellow Irish and Scottish officers, he plotted to assassinate the generalissimo. At the town of Eger, colonels loyal to Wallenstein were invited to an evening feast and when the diners had reached the drinking stage, Butler entered with twelve dragoons crying, 'Who is for the emperor?' The Irish and Scottish officers sprang up, drew their swords and, each taking up a candle from the table, cried, 'Long live the House of Austria.' Two of Wallenstein's lieutenants were cut down as they went for their weapons, while Wallenstein's brother-in-law defended himself desperately: his doublet of elkskin protected him from so many thrusts that his attackers thought he bore a charmed life, but he fell at last, pierced through the body.

The dragoons went immediately to Wallenstein's castle nearby. On the way they could hear the wails of the wives of the murdered officers who had learnt of the death of their husbands. Wallenstein had left his bed and had gone to the windows to ask the watch what the noise was. A dragoon, with his foot thrusting open the door, called out, 'Art thou the traitor who would deprive the emperor of his crown and kingdom?' Wallenstein stretched out his arms in silence, was pierced through his unflinching breast and sank upon the ground without a groan.

In the present huge exhibition there is little about the suspicions of Wallenstein's treachery and only some small sketches of his murder. There is no hint of the gratitude and rewards that Walter Butler received from the emperor for the deed, which, as a priest said at the time, 'made our country and our nation, otherwise quite unheard of here, most famous and well-known'. I wondered if my audience might turn on me for ascribing Butler's actions to loyalty and honour and throw me from the window. There was no dung heap outside. I looked. But no defenestration occurred – it would have made it very cold if a window had had to be broken.

20. *Jonathan Swift Building, Kilkenny College*

When I was at school, if one wanted to be alone – not so much for solitude but to read *Forever Amber* undisturbed, a book that was considered by the authorities to be likely to debauch our tender minds – one locked oneself in the lavatory until matron threatened sundry punishments through the keyhole.

How things have changed! In the new building that has been erected by Kilkenny College and is being opened this week with a fanfare of ministers of state there is, besides up-to-date classrooms and laboratories, a quiet room for student reflection. The building is named for the college's most distinguished past pupil, Jonathan Swift, who was a student here from the age of six until he went to Trinity. His memories of his schooldays are mixed: 'The confinement for ten hours a day to nouns and verbs, the terror of the rod, the bloody nose and broken shins but also the delicious holidays, the Saturday afternoons, and the charming custards in a blind alley.'

It must have been during those delicious holidays that the two best-known anecdotes about his life at Kilkenny College took place. 'I remember when I was a little boy, I felt a great fish at the end of my line which I drew almost to the ground. But it dropped in and the disappointment vexeth me to this very day and I believe was type of all my future disappointments.' The other anecdote recounts that, for the momentary glory of riding his own horse through Kilkenny, Swift spent all his money on a nag on its way to the slaughterhouse. Alas, the poor horse soon succumbed.

Kilkenny College was founded in or around 1667 by the Great Duke of Ormonde on land on the other side of the river from the castle. Only the hooded mouldings of the doorways remain of the original house that fronted onto John Street:

> a grey reverend pile of irregular and rather struggling design. The entrance to the schoolroom was from the street through huge oak folding doors gained by two grand flights of steps on each side that formed a generous platform before the entrance. There were gothic windows, gables, chimneys and spouts which jetted into the street to the annoyance of the passers-by in rainy weather while from the platform before the schoolroom entrance, lads of the college contrived further aggravations.

In 1782, a square three-storey building with a plain classical facade was put up to rehouse the school. Homan Potterton, who became director of the National Gallery, writes in his autobiography *Rathcormick*, 'I came to realize that it was beautiful ...' and goes on to describe the elaborate fanlight as 'a frilly trollop flaunting herself above the hall-door'. In 1973, Kilkenny College merged with the Collegiate Girls' School of Celbridge and moved to Newtown, a house on the edge of Kilkenny city. The Georgian house on the banks of the Nore was taken over by the county council.

When founding the college, the Duke of Ormonde wished the boys to be instructed in religion, virtue, learning in the Latin, Greek and Hebrew languages, as well as oratory and poetry.

Children with contagious diseases were to be sent home and those who damaged school property or rebelled against authority were only to be restored after 'exemplary discipline'. The school day was to begin at six o'clock and to go on to eleven, resuming in the afternoon from one o'clock to five o'clock. They were to have half-days on Thursdays and Saturdays. Up to the end of the eighteenth century, both the nobility and the people of the town educated their sons at the college. Kilkenny citizens paid only half-fees. Thus future dukes and lords mixed with future weavers, saddlers, merchants, a milliner and, of course, boys who went on to do law, medicine or into the army.

In 1689, the second Duke of Ormonde and the masters of the school were attainted for high treason by James II, who then endowed the school as a university with a rector, eight professors and two scholars. But the new foundation was only three months old when the Battle of the Boyne was lost and with it all the aspirations to university status, and it returned to being a school.

William Magee, who became Archbishop of York, was at school here in 1833. Like Swift he suffered a disappointment, 'his faith in the kindness of others was shattered when a big boy came up to him holding a fruit tart: "New boy, do you like tart?"

"Oh very much," said little Magee.

"Then," said the other, "Look at me eating one." '

(If these examples of serious disillusionment were part of the formation of the character of the great man, my character should be outstanding from the number and depth of disappointments I suffered at the academy for young ladies that I attended!)

However, in fiction things look very different when one reads *Fetches* by John Banim, the Kilkenny novelist. Tresham, a student of eighteen, enrols in the college in order to brush up on the classics, but he also dabbles in Rosicrucianism, a legendary and mystical fraternity involving the occult. His cupboard is piled with skulls and loose bones that he studies during his leisure. Though we are told he is a devoted classical student at the college, it doesn't seem to take up much of his time as he falls in love. He and his sweetheart wander in the college shrubbery, in spite of meeting up with a tall black figure topped by a fiery, red face of severe expression with eyes that flash and a mouth that leers. One would think this would be the indignant headmaster, but apparently it is some fiend, who throngs the lovers' paths with wraiths and 'fetches'. The story ends tragically with Tresham dying in his lover's arms as she meets a watery death herself.

Richard Stanihurst wrote of the first Kilkenny school that it had 'sprouted many proper impes'. But he was referring to the many distinguished scholars that have passed through its hallowed halls and will, we surmise, continue to do so.

21. *Freestone Hill*

The tale of Freestone Hill is as good as a mystery novel, though the corpse is distanced from the detective by five thousand years and the story of the sleuth is more interesting than that of the young female who was found lying in the configuration of an S, in a grave that had been marked for posterity by a mound of stones.

Freestone is a steep little hill, crowned by a single thorn tree, about six miles from Kilkenny city, overlooking the road to Dublin. From the summit one can see Mount Leinster and Slievenamon and down the valley of the Nore towards Thomastown. The burial cairn, under which the young lady was interred, was built by our pre-Celtic ancestors during the Bronze Age, but only remnants remain. The cairn was dismantled by the people of the Iron Age who had a fort up there and used the stones to build the defensive rampart that encircles the hill.

We know all this because a very distinguished German archaeologist did a dig here in 1947 and the reason why he came is both historic and curious. Dr Gerhard Bersu had taken part in excavations all over Europe, and by revolutionary methods that included meticulous examination of domestic waste was able to illuminate many facts about Iron Age settlements. In the 1930s, he had been the director of the Institute of Archaeology in Frankfurt, but being part Jewish, he was forced to leave and had gone to England. When war broke out he was interned as an enemy alien for the duration on the Isle of Man, though he was allowed to do several excavations there.

When the war was over, an English archaeologist, O.G.S. Crawford, came to Kilkenny, not to examine any of our ancient monuments, but to place a weekly order with a Kilkenny butcher, which would be dispatched to his home in Southampton, as he thought the meat from here would be superior to anything he could purchase there. While he was staying with Hubert Butler, he suggested that his friend Dr Gerhard Bersu, who was doubtful about how he would be received back in Germany, should be invited to Kilkenny while he explored the possibilities of working in Ireland.

Hubert Butler had latterly revived the Kilkenny Archaeological Society, which had been originally founded in 1849 by a Protestant clergyman, James Graves, but a few years later had become a national society and the headquarters moved to Dublin as the Royal Society of Antiquaries. The local society had withered and died until it was started again in 1945. With the arrival of Dr Bersu, members of the society suggested Freestone Hill as a likely site, and Dr Bersu took on the excavation.

While the excavation was in progress, the centenary of the Kilkenny Archaeological Society and therefore of the Society of Antiquitaries occurred and to celebrate this occasion, three days were planned in Kilkenny with twelve of the world's most eminent archaeologists in attendance. Hubert Butler was asked to put up a Dr Sprockhoff, an important German prehistorian, who had been sent to Norway by Himmler to dig a site that the

Nazis had linked to the Aryan origins of the German people. When Bersu heard that he was coming, he was outraged and said he could not meet him. He told Hubert that Sprockhoff had barred him from even reading in the archaeogical library when the Nazification of Germany had taken place. In the circumstances, Hubert felt that he could not have Sprockhoff to stay and the RSAI put him up in a hotel, where he was able to attend the celebratory centenary lunch with other archaeologists among whom were a Spanish fascist and an American McCarthyite – the English scholars had refused to come because of the presence of Sprockhoff. Neither Hubert nor Dr Bersu received an invitation.

Ironically, that weekend the RSAI brought the archaeologists to Freestone Hill, Sprockhoff, seeing Bersu there, went up to him and shook him warmly by the hand while congratulating him on the excavation and on the importance of his findings. Later Bersu said to Hubert, 'It is all right about Sprockhoff, he was very nice,' and some years later when a Festschrift was published to celebrate Sprockoff's sixtieth birthday, one of the contributors was Bersu. The only victim of the occasion was Hubert Butler, who missed the lunch and had boycotted the meetings, but at least retained the integrity of his convictions.

Since the forties, Irish archaeologists have looked again at Freestone Hill and have concluded that there was also a temple there built of the Romano-British type.

It being the time of the festival of Bealtaine, a friend and I climbed the hill preparing to meditate or at least feel the vibes of the past. The blackthorn sceoc that grows prominently on the highest point and is a landmark for miles around was smothered in delicately scented white blossoms, but we saw that the trunk had been sawn almost through. There seemed no rhyme or reason for this vandalism and I would not like to be in the shoes of the perpetrator when the gods take their revenge. As we examined the sceoc, there was a roar, or perhaps more truthfully a snort, and we looked up to find we were being watched by a huge white bull. Perhaps it was Finnbennach, the white bull of King Ailill, sent to guard this sacred spot against any further depredation.

22. Castle Oliver

On a foggy autumn day last week, I was eating a sandwich on the wooded slopes of Ballyhouras in Limerick. A sudden shaft of sunlight pierced the mist across the valley and there, looking as if it was floating on a cloud, was a fairy-tale pink castle with towers and turrets, which could only have been designed as detention centres for beautiful princesses until released by the right prince.

The Olivers of Clondofoy near Kilfinane in County Limerick had been here since the seventeenth century. In order to alleviate the effects of the Famine, Castle Oliver was built of the local sandstone in the Scottish baronial style by two sisters, nieces of the notorious Silver Oliver. It dominates this remote valley with vistas over the Golden Vale. The miniature fortresses that guard the gates would win prizes in a sandcastle competition and high on the hill behind is a romantic gothic folly also built of red sandstone.

The sisters married two Trenches, one of whom became Lord Ashtown and the castle continued to belong to the Trenches until 1978. After this it fell into disrepair, the interior was vandalized, the lead was taken from the roof, ivy covered the walls and the ceilings were propped up by tree trunks.

It was almost derelict when in 1998 a young Englishman, Nick Browne, saw and fell in love with it. His mother, who sounds most unlike other parents, said, 'Why not buy it?' Which he did. '*Ago Gratias Matri*' or in English, 'Thanks Mum' reads the painted scroll over the window in the hall. He had always had a fascination for old houses and instead of completing a more formal education, had learnt to replace slates, turn wood and act as his own glazier. So he was able to mend the roof, helped by the iron trusses that were a remarkable innovation of the original architect. Nick has meticulously restored the reception rooms and entirely rebuilt the great wooden staircase with its barley-sugar banisters. Outside he has planted trees and cleaned up the terrace with its unique pierced iron parapet. There is a fountain splashing into a pool and, not content with what he has, he has built his own folly, a grotto, or perhaps a hermitage if there are any hermits looking for a fern-filled home.

Castle Oliver is always connected with Lola Montez, the beautiful adventuress who became a celebrity. Her mother was the illegitimate daughter of Silver Oliver who in his will left her five hundred pounds. With this fortune she married Edward Gilbert, an army officer, and their only daughter was born in Ireland just before they left for India.

Lola was fifteen when she eloped with Lieutenant Thomas James, an Irish officer of the East Indian Company, 'a smart looking man with bright teeth and bright waistcoats' from Ballycrystal in Wexford. They were married by his brother, the rector of Rathbeggan in Meath and soon after sailed for India. Emily Eden, the sister of the governor general, records the sensation Lola caused when she came to Simla to stay with her mother. 'She is undoubtedly very pretty and such a merry unaffected girl.

She is only seventeen and is married to an officer fifteen years older than herself with 160 rupees a month and they are to pass their whole lives in India. No wonder at her mother's resentment at her having run away from school.'

However, Lola did not stick around for long and returned by herself in 1842 to England where James divorced her for adultery. From then on she called herself Lola Montez, a dancer from Spain. After her first engagement in London she received rave reviews for her looks but the critics said nastily that she knew more about other things than dancing or Seville.

She was, however, a great success in Paris, Berlin and Warsaw and had many affairs, including one with Liszt, though not for long, as she burst in on a dinner party he was holding and danced on the table until she sent a bowl of soup flying into the lap of a duke.

In Bavaria she was seen by the aged King Ludwig of Bavaria who had tea with her, became infatuated and pleaded with her to stay in Munich. He gave her an allowance and a house, and had her portrait painted and her foot modelled in marble, which he used as a paperweight.

He also made her a countess, which infuriated the Bavarian nobility. She wrote letters interspersing the contents of how much she loved him with how much she needed money; she also meddled in politics and in the promotion and demotion of officers. The Bavarians abhorred her, there were riots and in the end she was forced to leave and the king abdicated soon afterwards.

By the summer she was back in London, married to a young guardsman of twenty-one. His aunt had Lola arrested for bigamy, as the divorce from her first husband was never finalized. The marriage soon ran into difficulties anyway, as the guardsman was so fearful of her dreadful temper that he was always running away and was eventually drowned. Lola went to seek her fortune in the Americas and lived for a time in a gold-mining town, where she kept a pet grizzly bear that ungratefully bit her hand. She toured Australia, then turned to lecturing on beauty and died in New York at the age of forty-three.

Castle Oliver would have been a fitting background for this tempestuous beauty – though she was not the sort to hang around until the right prince turned up.

23. *Canon Carrigan*

It was a very hot day for cutting down the brambles and nettles in the ruined church of Coolcraheen in Kilkenny; only a youthful clergyman showed much energy as he swatted the horseflies that buzzed around us. 'More action, more action,' called Hubert Butler, the writer, from a chair that, in deference to his advanced years, we had carried across the fields for him. Then, unable to bear our lethargic efforts, he sprang up, seized a saw from the hand of an American poetess and cut down two elder trees. Spurred by this enthusiasm, Kevin Myers slashed at the nettles, and the singer, Nora Ring, who was drinking the cider that we had brought to sustain ourselves, called out that she could see the carving on the stone that had lain hidden for so long.

Hubert, with the help of Canon William Carrigan's *History and Antiquities of the Diocese of Ossory*, was directing our efforts to uncover the Purcell tomb dated 1629. On it was the coat of arms incorporating the heads of three boars and we were also searching for the pieces of the mural tablet that has a Latin verse with a pun on the name Purcell, which is the old French word for swineherd.

In those halcyon days when friends and neighbours would accompany Hubert on picnics and expeditions, he would consult 'Carrigan' as to our destination, and when he died he left the four volumes to me – now in this centenary year of its publication [1905], a comprehensive index has been brought out by the Canon Carrigan Centenary Committee of the Diocese of Ossory.

Canon Carrigan was born in Ballyfoyle in Kilkenny, the youngest son of a farmer. After being educated in St Kieran's in Kilkenny and in Maynooth, he was ordained in 1884. His curacies were in Kilkenny until he was transferred to Durrow in Laois, where he was made the parish priest in 1909, became a canon and died in 1924.

'A holy priest who wrote a book' was how one parishioner described him, and the four volumes are a remarkable life's work. He must have walked every townland in the county with his tape measure, for the dimensions of the antiquities are carefully written down and described in the one hundred and sixty-six notebooks that he filled. He gathered information on churches that were ruined or had disappeared, schools, old graveyards, inscriptions, raths, castles and ancient roads. He also wrote up the history and genealogy of the ancient families who lived in the neighbourhood. Equipped with his notebook, he would visit the Irish speakers and elderly people in the district to question them about the names, legends and hearsay of the area and thirty-seven of his annual vacations were spent studying manuscripts in the Public Record Office in Dublin.

With 'Carrigan' in hand, we went to look at the ogham stones built into the walls of Clara church and to test the clock stones that the sun is meant to strike at noon, but somehow our visits never coincided with the sun, the time and finding the clock stone. There was the gravestone put up by a gentleman in Gowran that reads:

> Both wives at once alive he could not have:
> Both to enjoy at once he made this grave.

Then there are the legends in the book, particularly that of St Kieran at Fertagh, who owned a pet lamb that used to wander the country and if anyone wanted to send a present they attached it to a string round the lamb's neck who brought it to St Kieran. Perhaps one day the gift was a pot of mint jelly for, alas, the lamb was stolen and eaten. The thief was soon exposed as the lamb complained loudly of its fate from the glutton's stomach. St Kieran was so angry about the robbery that he cursed Fertagh, saying, 'it would never be without a liar or a rogue till the end of time'.

After Carrigan had published his volumes, a booklet of one hundred and fifteen pages of criticisms was printed and there is particular reference to this incident that the author calls 'a ridiculous old druidical story which should not be committed to deathless type'. It is now believed that the detractor was the parish priest of Fertagh.

On another page there is the transcription of a letter from Bishop Brenan who fled from Waterford in 1673 as it was 'full of fanatics and furious Presbyterians', to take refuge with his friend the Archbishop of Armagh. But things were no better there and they had to 'take to their heels; the snow fell heavily mixed with hailstones which were very hard and large'. And though they found shelter in a garret, there was no fire. 'The running of the eyes of my companion and myself has not ceased,' he says sadly, 'and I feel that I shall lose more than one of my teeth so frightful is the pain it is giving me.'

One of my favourite anecdotes is of the raven that croaked in Irish, 'I slept in Dublin last night and the fair Lord is ruined.' The workmen immediately stopped work on Balleen Castle that was being built for the Lord Mountgarret and it was never completed.

Even without going to the sites, Canon Carrigan's book is a joy to read and now the index to the four volumes will make it much easier to study the history, archaeology and genealogy of the diocese.

24. *William Colles*

I don't have to dream that I dwelt in marble halls for I live near the city of Kilkenny in a house that was built by the owners of the marble works. There are marble pillars in my porch and there are marble flagstones in my kitchen, though these are not beautiful, being a dull black, and no mother-in-law ever asked for the secret of my shining floors. The marble is really the local limestone, which, when polished, becomes a handsome black, flecked with white fossil shells that look like jackdaws' eyes.

Two hundred and seventy-five years ago, William Colles wrote to the Royal Dublin Society that he now had ten saws cutting marble in his mills on the banks of the Nore at Maddoxtown. Previously the marble had been worked laboriously by hand. William's invention of machinery run by water for cutting and polishing was the first of its kind in Europe. A travel book written in 1748, possibly by Rufus Chetwode (whose greatest distinction was being the best prompter in the London theatre), went into rhapsodies: 'The finest piece of mechanism our eyes ever beheld. This engine, or rather different engines, do marvellous work by the help of the river. It is perpetually at work like a ship at sea by night as well as by day and requires little attention.' Another writer estimated that it did the work of forty-two men.

They certainly turned out some remarkable artefacts; cisterns, buffets – whatever they are – punchbowls, mugs of different dimensions and frames for looking glasses and pictures. Bishop Pococke also mentioned tea dishes and saucers. In Kilkenny there was a room lined with marble in imitation of wainscot. Indeed, such was the ingenuity of William Colles that he introduced a method for boring the marble and offered to supply the corporation of Dublin with tubes for water mains, but, alas, the men who made the pipes of wood, fearful of losing their trade, destroyed the marble on its arrival in the city. There was only one house, on Usher's Quay, which was fitted with marble downpipes.

William Colles had a mind that ranged widely over different subjects. In his youth, he had written several tragedies and he started a number of practical, if sometimes eccentric, schemes. One of his less successful ideas was using dogs turning wheels to weave linen, but he was commended for his engine for dressing flax and he had a cider mill that must have been of interest to the RDS, which was at this time encouraging apple growing. To amuse people he made a musical instrument like an Aeolian harp that played by itself when it floated on the river. I don't know if it was because of these ghostly tunes or the constant whirring of his inventions, but he was reputed locally to practise the black arts. As alderman and then mayor of Kilkenny, he was almost the only member of the corporation to be personally involved in the commerce of the city, the other city fathers being landed gentry.

The plan for a canal from Kilkenny to Inistiogue was enthusiastically supported by him, as he would have been able to use it for transporting his marble, thus saving him up to six shillings

a ton. The canal was dug from Kilkenny as far as Bennettsbridge
– the channel and one of the locks still exist. The construction
soon overran the budget and parliament refused to grant any
more funds until a boat was unloaded at the quay in Kilkenny.
William Colles made a bet that this could be done and amid
mock rejoicings a barge was dragged by horses along the bed of
the unfinished canal and its cargo of hides delivered. Some years
later, after more money had been given but nothing much had
happened, the scheme collapsed.

The marble works had numerous contracts for buildings in
the county and employed so many people that Colles claimed he
had banished the beggars from the streets of Kilkenny. The parish
priest said the locals paid more attention to the bell that started
their working day than they did to the bell that summoned them
to Mass. There is a rhyme that goes:

> Maddoxtown, Lavistown, and Lower Dunbell,
> Three little towns going straight to hell,
> For all they hear is Colles's bell.

William Colles built his house by his mills where there had
been an old abbey, but it was so close to the river that, when
there was a flood, the grandfather clock floated out of the front
door and, shortly after, the house was resited farther back on a
hill. The river was always a strong influence on the Colleses for
William's grandson, Abraham, found a book on surgery that had
been swept down in another flood from Kilkenny. He was so
impressed by this work that he became a surgeon and a distinguished professor of the newly formed Royal College. A fracture
of the wrist is named after him.

The marble works continued in the hands of the Colleses
until 1920. I have an old advertisement listing work done in six
cathedrals, at the public baths at Alloa and the carving of a monument to Cyrus W. Field, projector of the Atlantic Telegraph.

The mills still stand, but as picturesque ruins by their mill races. Kilkenny has replaced the marble paving stones and our pigs no longer dine out of marble troughs as they did in the eighteenth century, but most of the old buildings still have their marble windowsills, door frames and cornerstones.

IV

SOCIETY

Knowing Melo

PETER SOMERVILLE-LARGE

When my wife Gillian and I came to live in Kilkenny in the early 1990s, among the few people we knew in the area was Peggy Butler, widow of Melo's uncle, the philosopher and essayist Hubert Butler. Through Peggy we met Melo. We shared a love of travel, and a background of biggish houses. Like Melo, Gillian had a colonial past that included life on a tea estate and a restless wartime childhood.

We soon discovered that her friends were legion. After she had enlarged her little gate lodge to incorporate a new book-filled living room, her guests sat beside a cascade of pelargoniums that fell like a curtain in front of the large south-facing windows (gardening was one of her skills about which she was too modest). During her dinner parties we were always certain to encounter a succession of congenial new acquaintances. Other times we spent with her were filled with hours of gossip and humour. It was always a delight when she paid us a visit, since acquaintance with Melo was never uninteresting.

In her one published book, Diaries of Ireland: An Anthology 1590–1987 *(1998), she edited entries from thirty-eight diarists, most of whom were newcomers to Ireland and wrote in English. She was candid in her introduction: 'The diaries ... have been chosen principally because I myself have enjoyed reading them ... I cannot claim that this book gives a balanced view.' Her one diarist writing in Irish was Amhlaoibh Ó Súilleabháin, kept mostly in the third decade of the nineteenth century: 'He loved the language and was fearful it would soon be lost.'*

Melo offered an absorbing survey of Irish society and history ranging across four centuries. Wolfe Tone shivers off Bantry Bay: 'Last night it blew a heavy gale from the eastward with snow, so that the mountains are covered this morning, which will render our bivouacs extremely amusing.' Elizabeth Smith laments the effects of famine: 'I was shocked at our own school, no rosy cheeks, no merry laugh, little skeletons in rags with white faces and large staring eyes crouching against one another half dead.'

Elsewhere, Melo's humour creeps into her selections. The Earl of Cork gives Mrs Walley 'a pair of sea water green silk stockings, garters and Roses'. Mrs Freke moans about her husband, and her dreadful sea crossing to Ireland, chased by Algerian pirates. A weary Gemma Hussey eats a semi-edible meal at the Wicklow Cheviot Sheep Owners dinner dance in Blessington and endures interminable raffles for fertilizer and sheep dip. Many good books contain a stroke of luck, and Melo was able to include an unforgettable entry from Frank McEvoy, writing in 1958: '[Patrick] Kavanagh has come and gone: like the monsoon, the mistral, Hurricane Annie: things will never be quite the same again, even if it only meant that somebody told Lady Bellew to shut up, and went on to declare later that he hates Prods.'

If only there was more. With her humour and powers of observation, Melo did not write nearly enough. The Butler Society can possibly take some of the blame. It certainly offered entertainment for her friends. We particularly enjoyed our back-seat view of the triennial crisis of her life, the organization of the Butler Rally, which she undertook for many years. From around the world, crowds of Butlers assembled by Melo gathered in Kilkenny and enjoyed themselves. She managed every event with her usual efficiency, although from initial groans and forecasts of disaster, failure was always predicted. Tension would build. What new places could Butlers visit? Where could they be accommodated? The computer has broken down. How could buses be arranged? How many? Could they go down some particular drive to a castle? We were detached, having no Butler connections, except for my godmother Naomi Overend, who would arrive with her sister, Tot, in an ancient Rolls-Royce. In her nineties, Naomi never missed a rally and probably gave Melo more trouble than the other Butlers put together.

For many years we followed her accounts of hardship-travels to destinations where few tourists were to be seen. She went around the world in the spirit of Victorian exploration and we wished her and her equally intrepid friend, Diana Merilees, who often accompanied her, the blessings of a good tweed skirt. Timbuktu, which she considered only fairly interesting; Assam, with its Naga villages where she encountered retired headhunters; the eastern fringes of China, near to Tibet, whose bamboo woods were inhabited by pandas, were among the places she visited. She trekked to remote parts of the Argentine in pursuit of Butlers and to Marib in the Yemen where she mused that it might be an adventure to be captured by a tribesman and held for ransom in the spirit of The Sheikh. *In 2001, she planned a visit to the Northwest Frontier and Tora Bora, but her timing was not good. The planned trip had to be aborted since it was only days before the American invasion of Afghanistan.*

I believe the journey that touched her most was her return to Sri Lanka where she had spent a seminal part of her childhood at a time when it was known as Ceylon. She loved her rediscovery of that beautiful island, and her recollections would have formed the basis for a vivid travel book.

25. *An Irish Game*

One of Alice's adventures in Wonderland was playing croquet with the Queen of Hearts; her ball was a hedgehog that would unroll itself to crawl to the safety of the other side of the pitch, while her mallet was a resentful flamingo. Alice found 'it was a very difficult game indeed', a statement with which I can concur even without having an animated croquet set. My mallet may not twist 'itself round and look me in the face with a puzzled expression', but my partners' often do and they yearn for the authority of the Queen of Hearts so as to be able to give the command: 'Off with her head!'

I do not know if there will be much call for decapitation, except in their hearts, from the women competitors who are taking part in the World Women's Golf Croquet Championships that are being held in Dublin. Forty competitors from nine different countries will battle it out at the Carrickmines Club and at the Herbert Park Club. Egypt has dominated all previous championships and the current World Champion will be here defending her title. She is Nahed Hassan, a practising lawyer married with two children who has been playing since 1974.

Golf croquet is a modified version of the traditional game now known as association croquet. In golf croquet, a turn is a single stroke and a point is scored by the side whose ball is first through each hoop, while in association croquet extra strokes can be gained by hitting other balls, and when a ball goes through a hoop. The winner is the side that goes first through all the hoops. Golf croquet, which was devised before the First World War, is now growing rapidly in popularity because, though fiercely competitive, it is more interactive and the rules are simpler than association croquet, though there is still the importance of tactics that defines this devious game. In the rulebook, Rule 14 on 'Behaviour' has now been replaced by Law 14 on 'Etiquette', which is only right and proper!

As a game that was devised in Ireland, croquet should be one of our Gaelic sports – possibly with an extra syllable it could have been Croquet Park! There was a time when it was played at Lansdowne Road, which, when it was first laid out, featured a croquet lawn as well as a rugby ground. In 1834, the game was invented and first played by the Macan family at a house called Greenmount near Castlebellingham in County Louth. Denis Kirwan from Castle Hackett, who was courting and eventually married Anne-Margaret Macan, was so enthusiastic that he took it back to his home in Galway and from there introduced it to the palace in Tuam where the Protestant bishop and his family became keen players. Soon afterwards it was taken up in the big houses of County Meath where George Pollok founded the first croquet club at Oatlands near Navan.

The game spread round the world: in fact one might say it changed the world. In Russia, Trotsky was returning from a game of croquet when he found his father had confiscated a cow from a wretched peasant and this act converted him to socialism, even though his father returned the cow to the peasant. What would have happened to the revolution in Russia if Trotsky had not been croqueted? In the United States, the twelfth president, Rutherford Hayes, was very fond of the game and spent $6 of government funds purchasing some good-quality croquet balls. He was later criticized for this outrageous expense and told he should repay the country out of his own pocket. Tolstoy had it as a game of romance. Anna Karenina went to a croquet party in hopes of seeing Vronsky. Unfortunately, he was at home doing his accounts and Anna never did get to play, in spite of saying that she enjoyed the game. The other players were two ladies and their adorers; one of them, Stremov, is described as 'a most amiable man and a devoted croquet player'.

My father at the age of eighty took up the game. Ignoring the indignant squeaks of his family, he turned the tennis court into a croquet lawn. He played summer and winter, hail, rain or shine, and whoever was staying in the house was expected to play with him. Through constant practice and natural talent my father became a good but ferocious player, terrorizing any timid opponent into cowering in the bushes pretending to look for their ball, which had been smacked off the court. There was no question of leniency to a beginner. He had many similarities, now I think of it, to the Queen of Hearts.

After a few years, he thought his game could do with some improvement and went off to a hypnotist in Dundalk. We questioned him closely as to what had happened. The hypnotist had never heard of croquet, but decided after some discussion that it was much the same as golf. He had not been able to put my father into a trance, but told him it would be as effective if he completely relaxed and concentrated his mind on success. My father told us that though disappointed not to be hypnotized, he thought meditation was probably as good. We hoped that from then on we would see him sitting in the lotus position on a mat among the croquet hoops doing a bit of meditating, but he seemed to think one session had done the trick and I have to say I reached the same conclusion after my father had defeated me in eight consecutive games. He would have enjoyed going to watch the Women's World Championships in Carrickmines, where he would have hoped to pick up a few hints on future tactics to further terrorize his opponents.

26. *Ancestral Portraits*

'Did you hear that Billy got nine million for the house and two hundred acres?'

'Oh, I heard fifteen million and the man who bought it sold it for twenty million to a developer the next week.'

'Where are they going to live?'

'They bought a few acres for the horses and have a site with a fabulous view, but they can't have many windows because Billy insisted on bringing the ancestors with him and they are huge – you remember that one of the chief justice in his robes: it's more than life-size, as is the one of his wife and she must have been a fine figure of a woman.'

'Family pictures are a problem,' Patrick, our host, says, as he offers around slices of toast to go with the pâté.

'I left the ugliest ones behind and they are hung in The Uncle Sampson's Snug, which is one of the bars that the golfers can go to when they come off the course. Uncle Sampson is whirling round in his grave. Unlike the rest of the family, he was a rabid teetotaller. I am surprised he doesn't haunt the place.'

The house where I am dining is new. Patrick can see the velvety green grass of what had once been the Big Meadow and is now the ninth hole from the window of his dressing room (the architect has looked at Patrick very strangely since he said he must have a dressing room – I think he has decided that he is a transvestite). And if he goes to the spare room he can get a glimpse of a corner of the great, grey, granite pile that his forbear built two hundred years ago.

In the dining room, the mass of pink roses arranged in the centre of the table has dropped a few petals amongst the preponderance of silver and glass. Boots, the old black Labrador, mooches uneasily across to the fireplace, his claws rattling and sliding over the varnished floorboards. On the walls, closer together than they ever were in life, hang portraits of gentlemen in periwigs and ladies in crinolines. Owing to the ceiling being somewhat lower than what they are used to, they no longer look down on their descendants but watch their every mouthful.

Patrick's wife explains: 'We gave the architect the list of all the things we could not do without, like a room to dry the dogs and where Patrick can clean his guns. There is a boudoir for me, where I keep my computer and look at my emails. Then upstairs we have a suite of rooms that can be converted into a self-contained flat for a keeper when we get too old.

'Oh yes, power showers in all the bathrooms. I prefer a bath myself, but the children said we must have these showers. Poor old Aunt Joan was hit straight between the shoulder blades when she leaned over to turn on the taps and cracked two ribs.'

When we have wiped the last crumbs of cheese delicately off our fingers with our napkins and Patrick has brought out the heavy glass decanter of port, the ladies withdraw for a tour of the house. In the drawing room, the curtains, with plain pelmets, are expensively lined and the colour almost, but not quite, picks out the blue in the faded chintz that covers the oversized fat armchairs and sofas. 'I don't want the place to look like a hotel and the covers were perfectly good, just a little worn from the dogs lying on them.' Mirrors surrounded by ornate gold frames reflect a collection of miniatures, and the grandfather clock with the paint on its face, now cracked into tiny lines, looks like an ancient butler standing guard at the door.

Our heels clack across the hall on the quarry tiles.

'Under-floor heating, such a luxury, but there are solar panels in the roof as we thought we ought to be environmentally friendly. It is so lovely being warm, I don't think I wore a vest once last winter, and in the old house I used to put on at least two and sometimes three and even then I was always cold.'

From the hall we go into the kitchen with its scarlet Aga.

'I told Patrick that I would not move without my Aga and he gave me this one for a ruby wedding present. No, we never boil sheeps' heads on it now – the dogs have tins. Boots prefers chicken and Minnie likes beef. The wooden worktops, cupboards and shelves, we designed ourselves. They are made from our own timber. The beech tree from behind the old walled garden, if you remember it – there is a driving range there now. Don't you think Patrick was clever to have thought up these built-in kennels for the dogs? Minnie, stop that – friends! Friends! Oh, naughty Minnie – she didn't draw blood did she? ...

'The conservatory is through here where we have most of our meals among the geraniums – so different to how we lived before when we huddled round the Aga in that dark old kitchen listening to the snap of mouse traps and the drip, drip of water.'

As I say my goodbyes, I ask about the portrait of the progenitor of the family that had hung in the hall of the big house.

'Sold. I never liked the old reprobate. He came to Ireland with nothing and ended up with forty thousand acres, which he had procured by foul rather than fair means. I suppose I should be grateful …' A helicopter flies overhead towards the golf course, drowning all speech.

27. The Duchess of Devonshire

In the film *The Duchess*, I saw a familiar hat. It was a glorious brimmed creation decorated with ostrich feathers that perched on the duchess's curls at an angle that belied gravity.

My familiarity stemmed from having worked as a secretary for Agnew's, the London art dealers in Bond Street. My employer wrote a book, or to be quite truthful, as I could not interpret his shorthand, I wrote a book on the history of the firm. The most sensational chapter was about a painting by Gainsborough of the Duchess of Devonshire that came up for sale in Christie's in 1876. It had a questionable provenance, being sold by a silk merchant who had bought it from a picture restorer and had belonged to an unknown Miss Magennis at the beginning of the nineteenth century. The Duke of Devonshire of the time claimed it did not portray his great-aunt and the artist Millais said Gainsborough was not the artist.

However, the general public was captivated by the exquisite painting, as was William Agnew who successfully bid 100,100 guineas, then the highest sum ever given for a picture at auction.

Agnew's put it on exhibit and as *The Times* wrote, 'it might be supposed that some great lady is holding a reception and this, in fact, is pretty much what is going on for all the world comes to see the duchess and is conquered by her fascinating beauty'.

Three weeks later when the caretaker came to open up, the picture had vanished, leaving the empty frame. There was a tremendous furore, but the only clue that Scotland Yard could find was the marks of a chisel to lever up a window. William Agnew said it was 'a public outrage more than a private calamity'. He offered a thousand pounds for its return, but it was not until seven months later that he received a letter announcing that the picture was in America and that if £3000 in gold were handed over, the duchess would be returned. The writer of the letter pointed out that the resultant publicity would more than cover the costs of the ransom. Enclosed in the envelope were strips cut from the edge of the picture that matched the remnant in the frame.

This letter was cautiously answered through the personal columns of *The Times*, but negotiations petered out when Agnew's proved reluctant to hand over the money. The actual thief was Adam Worth, a notorious American criminal of the 1870s who was already a successful bank robber, jewel thief and forger. With his ill-gotten gains he had bought a house in Piccadilly, a yacht and a string of racehorses. He had once picked the pocket of the lawyer to whom he had just paid $1000 for defending him. It is said that Worth determined to steal the Gainsborough because the duchess reminded him of his Irish girlfriend, Kitty Flynn, but he was also planning to use it to bargain the release of his brother from prison, but then found his brother had been let go on a legal technicality. The theft had been remarkably simple: all he had done was climb on the shoulders of a brawny accomplice and jemmy open the window into the gallery.

Twenty-five years later news came that the picture could be

returned, so in 1901 the then chairman of the firm, Morland Agnew, sailed for America to meet with the detective agent, Pinkerton, in Chicago. At an appointed time, they waited in a hotel room. There was a knock at the door, a messenger entered and handed over a brown paper roll, then turned on his heel and left the room. Morland Agnew took out his knife, cut the string and unrolled the picture; it was the long-lost Gainsborough – somewhat battered from her ordeal, 'but still of immense value and of the highest interest'. Morland Agnew went at once to purchase waterproof paper and two light boards with which he wrapped the painting. He said blithely that he took no special precautions to safeguard the canvas but hung it on a peg in his compartment on the train back to New York. On the steamer home, he padded a cupboard with pillows and told only the captain, the purser and a well-known Catholic prelate that the picture was on board.

The Gainsborough *Duchess of Devonshire* was sold almost immediately and went back to the States, but has since been acquired by the Devonshire estates and now hangs in Chatsworth. Having seen the film of the Duchess of Devonshire's unhappy marriage, I wonder if the picture would prefer the old life as a gangster's moll!

28. *Emergency*

There is an office somewhere in Ireland – I like to think of it in
a bunker deep under St Stephen's Green that can only be entered
by pressing a code on the hand of James Joyce's statue – where
they look at the likely scenarios of future disasters. This office
has issued a handbook entitled *Preparing for Major Emergencies*, so
that if these happen we will remain calm and confident in the
knowledge that there are plans afoot to deal with the situation.

There are eight specific catastrophes described in thirty-nine
pages in Irish and then, just in case anyone has difficulty with
our native tongue, thirty-nine pages in English. One of these
booklets has been sent to every household. The paper involved
must have used up a small forest of trees, thus increasing global
warming, which melts the ice caps and causes universal flooding.
Fortunately, this is the first emergency covered in the handbook.
For flooding, fire, chemical spills, explosions and suspicious pack-
ages, the handbook advises one to 'keep calm and think before
acting', then, if possible, leave the scene. In my haste to get away,

without doing a bit of 'thinking', I might jump from a window on the eighth storey or try to swim my way to safety – I am not very good at swimming so I hope that a reader of page thirteen will notice my struggles and ring 999 or 112 and 'not leave it to another person to call'.

There are four pages decorated with tasteful tones of orange on 'Nuclear Incidents'. The Office of Emergency Planning has obviously put in a lot of work behind the scenes on this one, for it says, 'There is a plan – The National Emergency Plan for Nuclear Accidents – in place to deal with any radiation that could affect Ireland.' When I read this, I raced off to find my iodine tablets that were sent out several months after the last radiation incident. I know they are somewhere handy, but I have not yet found them.

Anyway, there is no mention of iodine tablets in the present plan. Instead we are told, 'Go in, stay in, tune in' – the information given is very soothing. In the first place, 'incident' sounds much less serious than 'accident'. And apparently the prevailing westerly winds are unlikely to blow radioactive dust towards us, which will anyway have been diluted by distance so the radiation doses should not be high enough to cause any immediate health results. Oh, it might contaminate the vegetables in my garden. I can't say I grow a cornucopia of fruit and vegetables and what there is is mostly devoured by slugs and caterpillars. After an 'incident' will they glow in the dark?

However, I have a booklet issued in the fifties by the Civil Defence that is much more alarmist, though no help to Irish speakers as, except for the title *Bás Beatha*, it is written entirely in English. There are entrancing illustrations of a young lady with elegant legs, high heels and a dainty apron tied about her slender waist. She behaves with great sang-froid, placing tinned meat and fish, raisins and salad oil, etc., into her store cupboard, filling the bath with water and putting food wrappings in a dustbin.

A less glamorous lady has to preserve eggs in water glass and churn butter before valiantly tackling a fire with a mop. The men illustrated are not of the same heroic mould, but have panicked and are pictured crouching beside a chimney breast or under the stairs. This cowardly behaviour does not do them much good as we see them suffering from radiation sickness, a fractured arm, getting mouth-to-mouth respiration or being crushed after crawling away from a fire.

There is another nasty situation that can happen and is not covered by the Office of Emergency Planning. It is being attacked in one's own home. Luckily, I have a booklet covering this subject. It does not say who issued this useful information, which is titled *Notes on the Defence of Irish Country Houses*. From the content, it must have been published around 1900. It is, I hope, rather too histrionic for the present day as it specifies an assault by fifty resolute men. Heavy library books, it suggests, can be part of the defence and it is very keen on firearms (revolvers should be reserved for hand-to-hand fighting).

The author is deeply suspicious of any piano tuner who calls by. It is nice to think that the householders, armed to the teeth and worn out with vigilance duties, should still be aware that their piano is out of tune. Apparently, a piano tuner is likely to disable the piano's owners and let in confederates who are not piano tuners. I do not have a piano so this is one less thing to worry about. The booklet urges that a constant watch should be kept at all times by one who moves at night on rubber-soled shoes, presumably carrying a firearm. I can't go as far as that, but sometimes on dark evenings I look under the beds and in the hot cupboard. Mostly, I just clump around in clogs hoping I will be mistaken for a heavyweight boxer. I once armed myself with Great-Uncle Gerald's ceremonial sword, but it became caught up in a curtain that it brought down on my head.

Even I don't think that there is a need to equip myself with hand grenades as the book recommends, nor do I think a nuclear attack is going to happen (by the way, if you are caught by a nuclear explosion, throw yourself flat on the ground with your hands under your body, protect your head and back of neck with anything you may be carrying). At this moment in time, emergencies seem less fearful than during the last hundred years, or perhaps it is the semantics. It occurs to me that World War II in Ireland was called The Emergency. What is the Office of Emergency Planning really cooking up?

29. Houses that Have Never Been Sold

What is it like to be watched by the ancestors in the dark oil paintings hanging on the walls? Is one ever-conscious of the mothers-in-law who were the chatelaines in the previous generations? When one hears a noise on the stair, is it the footstep of Great-grandfather's ghost going up to shoot himself in the blue room? Or is it a mouse?

Elizabeth Bowen wrote, 'Why fight to remain in a draughty mansion, in a demesne shorn of most of its land, far from neighbours, houses, shops and golf courses?' Remarkably, there are still about a hundred of these houses built over two hundred years ago that have never been sold by the families.

The long avenue winds through the trees to Monksgrange with its attractive facade of dressed granite. The wings on either side give an added graciousness and welcome to the exterior. On the hall-door steps four-year-old Edward Hill is playing with a toy tractor, the tenth generation to have lived in the house, say his grandparents, Rosy and Jeremy Hill.

Originally this land had belonged to the monks of Duiske Abbey in Graiguenamanagh, hence its name. But some time after the dissolution of the monasteries, it was acquired by the Hollow Sword Blade Company, a London merchant company, who sold it to John Richards of Raheen near Enniscorthy, in 1742. By 1769, his son had built the present house. Since then it has gone through various vicissitudes, such as 1798 when the Richardses could see the battles of Oulart and Kilthomas from their hall door, while the rebels were massing on the hillside behind. However, John Kelly, 'the Boy from Killane', was a neighbour and, even though he was a Catholic, a member of the vestry of the Protestant church where John Richards was curate. Kelly told them he could protect the house if the family would retreat to Bath. Accordingly, they left with such speed that Mrs Richards, with her baby under one arm and a silver tea urn under the other, had to run down the avenue after the carts.

Similarly, in 1922, Edward Richards Orpen was advised by a prominent republican, Mylie Fenlon, who had worked on the estate as a carpenter, that the house would not be burnt if they, too, left the country. Edward, who was pro-Treaty, was one of the founder members of Fine Gael and was a senator from 1942 to 1945. On his return from England, Edward Richards Orpen set up a furniture workshop, which produced modern, simple furniture out of native hardwoods. Examples of the excellent work done there are scattered throughout the house, particularly in a bedroom furnished entirely from the workshop. Though this innovative enterprise closed in 1933, the workshop, in which all the machinery survives, can still be seen.

Jeremy Hill, who had been a pilot with Aer Lingus, inherited the house from his uncle. At the time he was living with his Australian wife, Rosy, outside Melbourne. 'It was very lovely there, the children liked their schools, I was working and my parents were just round the corner,' Rosy says. 'But Jeremy said that he was coming back to Monksgrange, so we just had to pack up and come too.' She adds, 'A rat ran across the front steps when we arrived and I wondered what had I let myself in for. There were not only live rats, we kept finding their corpses when we moved the furniture or even opened drawers.'

'The house was in good condition structurally,' Jeremy tells me. 'After the failure of the furniture company, my uncle had had American paying guests, which meant putting in lots of bathrooms – a rarity for houses like this in the thirties.' Rosy says reflectively, 'It was after about ten years when the children were almost grown up that I really felt myself part of the place; I think it was when I took up gardening and I got my hands dirty in the earth of Monksgrange. Now, I am sure it was the right decision to come here.'

The Edwardian gardens slope up the mountain. The Hills, who have put so much work into them, have made a part into a park to display sculpture. They also run the Norman Art Gallery in the room of a wing of the house, where they have several shows a year of living artists. Rosy works as a psychologist for the Eastern Health Board in Enniscorthy and their son Ben has taken over the farm, while Jeremy breeds thoroughbreds – his mother was Charmian Hill who owned Dawn Run.

'It was mostly the women who came to Monksgrange who have kept the place going,' Jeremy says. His great-grandmother was born in Kansas and as a child was almost on the front line during the American Civil War; she had been instructed to be ready to harness up a cart and drive westwards if shells started to fall on the farm. Her father inherited Monksgrange and, feeling vulnerable in what is after all a fairly isolated place, he mounted a swivel gun in the upstairs front window.

As I leave, I look at the view where so much history has taken place and think how green and peaceful it is today.

'It takes about three hours to cut the grass,' Sally St George told me as she stopped the mower to greet me. The lawns are surrounded with herbaceous borders that are colourful with phloxes, dahlias and penstemons.

Kilrush is a handsome square house in front of a ruined tower house, which was where the St Georges lived for almost two hundred years after they first came to Kilkenny. In 1650, Captain Arthur St George of Athlone was granted the land and castle, which had four storeys and wings on each side. An inventory from 1750 lists the curtains, beds, chairs, tables and tapestries, which would have both been decorative and given some insulation to the walls. They were valued at £6 16s. each. The most costly item in the castle was the brewing furnace, which was worth £20.

Just about that time, the St Georges had thought of commissioning a house from Francis Bindon, who had already designed three of the grandest houses in Kilkenny. There is a plan where one can see the elaborate grounds that were envisaged with 'arcaded places of rest' in the shrubberies. Francis Bindon had been a friend and had painted a portrait of General Richard St George. There is another portrait of St George Ashe, who as provost of Trinity had been tutor to Jonathan Swift; a letter from a friend of Swift says that St George Ashe conducted the marriage service for Swift and Stella.

It was not until 1813 that the present house was built to the design of the architect William Robertson of Kilkenny. It is a well-proportioned Regency building with a flight of four cut-stone steps up to a Doric door case.

Sally was working with bloodstock in Tipperary when she met Richard. 'When Richard first brought me on a visit, the hall was a dank, dark green and the whole house felt and was damp; after two days I could wring out my woollen skirt that had been hanging in my room,' she says. 'After I married and came to live here, I used to wear rubber boots when I cooked as there was only an old electrical stove that sparked and hissed as its connections were faulty, so I was terrified I might get electrocuted.'

Unusually for a house this size, there were two bathrooms, the original one and the one 'with the bath that my mother-in-law hijacked. She said that as she had two children and both her mother and mother-in-law lived in the house she could not manage with only one bath. When she heard there was a bath in transit at Kilkenny station, she persuaded the stationmaster to redirect it to Kilrush.' The family in Cappoquin who were eagerly waiting to receive the bath are still indignant about the abduction.

The wallpaper in the drawing room was put up in 1840. Patterned with leaves, it has faded to a charming grey. The dining room, too, has its original dull maroon and silvery grey wallpaper and much of the furniture was bought when the house was built. Over the inner hall, the lighting for the stair hall is from an elegant glazed dome.

'We are grateful to the county council, the Heritage Council and the Georgian Society who helped with redoing the roof lately,' Richard says. 'We had buckets everywhere to catch the leaks. Once a bird nested in a gutter that runs under the roof and the water poured down the stairs.'

For a few years the St Georges ran a country-house guest house, but now they do lunch or dinner for tours. As well as farming, they breed thoroughbreds. Their younger son, Henry, works in London while the elder is working for Eaton Sales in Kentucky. One day he will return, they hope, to be yet another Arthur St George of Kilrush.

'It is not a daunting house; I was never intimidated by its size,' Tina Kavanagh says. 'I was twenty-four when we came to live here and we had a year-old baby.'

Borris must have one of the most enchanting set-ups in Ireland. The house looks across parkland and woods to the Blackstairs Mountains, which are constantly changing colour. These were the ancestral lands of the MacMurrough Kavanaghs, the ancient kings of Leinster. In 1590, Morgan Kavanagh is described as living at 'ye olde castle' at Borris. The family was politically astute and canny enough to marry into the powerful Butler family, so that they remained in possession of 30,000 acres throughout the Penal days and lived in a semi-fortified mansion very similar to the ones at Portumna and Rathfarnham. At the beginning of the nineteenth century, they employed the architects Richard and Vitruvius Morrison to smarten it up. The facade was given its Tudor Gothic appearance and the interior has delightfully exuberant plasterwork with festoons of swirling acanthus leaves and eagles holding garlands of flowers up with their outspread wings.

Andrew's great-great-great-grandfather was the remarkable Arthur MacMurrough Kavanagh, who was born with no arms or legs but could ride in the special saddle that is still in the hall at Borris, and was also a fine shot and fisherman. As a youth, his mother sent him with his brother and a tutor to travel in Russia, down through the Middle East and on to India. When he returned to Ireland, his elder brothers had both died so he inherited Borris. Here in the yard, he held court with his tenants under a huge oak tree, his pet bear beside him. Alas the oak died, but one of its acorns was planted and is now a twenty-foot-high tree. He was a Member of Parliament for Carlow and had his own yacht on the river Barrow so that he could sail over to London and tie up by the steps of the House of Commons.

Three of Andrew and Tina's children, including their son Morgan, live with their families on the estate.

'No, we have not altered much,' Tina says. 'In fact, we have bought back furniture that had been sold. When we first came here, we called the kitchen Cockroach City. It was in the original dining room, to which we have changed it back.' The kitchen is now next to it in a room at the front of the house. They have also restored the ballroom so that it can be used for concerts or as a theatre.

There have been problems with the roof since the Morrisons concealed it with a parapet, but latterly it has been completely redone, which cost a horrific amount even with the generous assistance of the Heritage Council.

As we go up the handsome staircase with its heavy mahogany banister, Tina tells me that the carpet was made for the house in the Abbeyleix factory in the nineteenth century. 'I darned it some time ago, but I must get out my needle and do some more work on it.'

At the head of the stairs there are two charming portraits in oval frames. Tina adds, 'I have just had them cleaned. They are the wedding portraits of Walter Kavanagh and his wife.' The ancestors smile, knowing that the family motto of *Síocháin agus Fairsinge* (Peace and Plenty) still holds good.

30. *Perfume*

My birthday this year was marked by a number of fragrant gifts, such as bath salts, body lotion and talcum powder. I suppose that this is a hint that I am suffering from body odour, but as my water pipes have been in a woeful state since the frost, there is not much I can do with bubble bath in a bucket. Against the time when running water is returned to me, I have made an inventory of my perfumed bath products from Christmases and birthdays past – I can smell of lavender, verbena, geranium, lemon tree, basil, jasmine and wild Chilean rose. Or if I prefer to be mistaken for a fruit salad, there are green apples, pomegranate, avocado and orange. My breath can be sweetened by peppermint and my hair smells of the ocean wave – I wish there was more wave to my hair and less of the wild, windblown, salty look.

One of the greatest changes in Ireland in the last fifty years must be people-smell. It used to be that they smelled not unpleasantly but of themselves: a tinge of turf smoke, tobacco, old cornflakes, Brylcreem, carbolic and hard work. Not so long ago, bathrooms were a rarity and even my family, who lived in a large house, had only one bathroom and that was halfway down the back stairs. The water was heated by the Ideal boiler situated far far away in the kitchen that had to be fed with care, as it was temperamental and if it took umbrage would sulk for days. Having an Aga and an Ideal boiler in the house was like owning a couple of temperamental dogs as they had to be cosseted, fed with anthracite, riddled twice a day, and only too often did they burn the hand that fed them.

For the first dance I went to, my mother suggested I use Johnson's baby powder because she said it attracted gentlemen callers as it would bring back happy memories of their babyhood. This was not good advice; nobody I met wanted to be reminded of their life in nappies so I am still an unclaimed treasure.

Becoming more sophisticated, I bought a tiny blue bottle of *Soir de Paris* shaped like the Eiffel Tower, which I dabbed behind my ears and imagined I was Audrey Hepburn (though I did rather wonder if she also bought her scent in Woolworths). Alas, it turned no heads when I swept down the staircase into the crowded hall, but at least I didn't now descend in a cloud like the prophet Elijah, which was what happened when I wore the Johnson's powder, as my younger brother and sister pointed out.

A long time ago, I came from India overland, camping out in the desert with very little water to drink, let alone use for washing, so I was pleased to reach Beirut, which at that time was a rich city by the sea known as the Paris of the Levant. I looked up a diplomat, a friend of a friend of a friend, and gratefully accepted the invitation to stay. That evening there was a dinner party – I did my best with the only clean dress in my suitcase and gave all my other clothes to the maid to be washed. In the middle of dinner, she came in to the dining room and asked my hostess in stentorian tones if she could have some money to buy soap. Giving a sniff and turning her eyes to me, she explained, 'We have a very dirty woman staying.'

31. *Reptile Village*

'Here be dragons' is not a phrase I would connect with the small village of Gowran in County Kilkenny, but there I was, like St George, facing up to a dragon that was making its way determinedly towards me. His head was fringed with spikes, his scaly body was armed with pointed barbs and his feet ended in scimitar-like claws, while his tail was stout and long and itself could be a weapon. I, unprotected, with not even a spear to hand, contemplated flight or at least backing off from a close encounter. 'He's friendly enough, a wee dote, really.' The dragon gave me a basilisk stare that froze the marrow in my bones; or would have if we had been the same size, but he was about a foot long and I am considerably larger in every direction.

One would not think that reptiles could be so fascinating, or perhaps mesmerizing is the appropriate word, but I cannot keep away from this most unusual zoo. The collection is housed in the back of a disused garage on the edge of Gowran with about a hundred and fifty animals on view.

The owner and creator of the Reptile Village, James Hennessy, comes from Callan. When he was fourteen, he was given a turtle that he still has – this sparked his interest in reptiles. At school, he instigated a frog race for Open Day and when he grew up he travelled the world to study the natural habitats of the reptiles. He did research in Cuba, India, Senegal, Venezuela and North Africa. His is a conservation zoo so most of his reptiles and amphibians have been bred in captivity. Many have been bred by James himself, including Conehead Iguanas, White-lipped Pit Vipers, Nile Monitors, Frilled Dragons, Cuban Knight Anoles and chameleons, as well as other rare and endangered species. He only breeds animals that he knows will find good homes in other zoos or with knowledgeable reptile enthusiasts. Alice, the boa constrictor, a television celeb who appeared on RTÉ wrapped around the Rose of Tralee, produced twenty-one babies (boa constrictors do not lay eggs), each only the length of a pencil and as thick as one's little finger, but their scaly skin has the same perfect pattern as an adult. James's assistant found them so enchanting that he took three of the babies home to live with him.

I grew up in Sri Lanka where snakes were common; St Patrick and I are as one in our dislike of serpents. The only compensation for coming to live in cold muddy Ireland was that there were no snakes. But here behind glass, one can look safely at their sinuous, graceful movements and admire the beauty of the different-coloured scales – what could be smarter than the Royal Python from Africa, which has a black skin decorated with a brown geometrical diamond motif? Design students should come here to study the subtlety of the different patterns and hues.

The glass-fronted enclosures are quite small. James Hennessy tells me that reptiles are not ones for broadening their minds with travel and in the wild they remain in their own defined area, so are happy with not much space. As all the reptiles in his care look sleek and glossy – almost as if they had been polished by a shoeshine boy – I feel the life of couch potato must suit most of his charges. A black eel-like creature opens a brilliant pink mouth as I pass, in what looks like a yawn, but as it is underwater it must be thoughts of lunch.

One of the concerns of keeping a reptile is not to feed them too much or too often – a full-grown python can live without food for a year. Here the animals are fed farm-bred rats, mice, rabbits, ducks and chickens that are bought frozen from a nearby pet-food farm.

There are a lot of myths about reptiles; the Gila Monster, it is alleged, if it catches you in its jaws, will not loosen its grip until the sun sets. There is an apocryphal story that a hoop snake will bite its own tail, form an inflexible circle and roll down a hill. But even in real life they have some remarkable habits, such as James Hennessy's Nile Monitor, which had an immaculate conception and laid two fertile eggs – the first time this has been recorded. There are geckos, small lizards with the ability to self-amputate their tails if they are under attack from predators. One of these species of lizard has webbed feet, which makes it appear to fly when jumping among the branches in a forest. A cousin, the Crested Gecko, has the most enviable eyelashes.

While I am passing, a Tegus, a large South American lizard, was doing its daily exercise round its enclosure until it fell into the pool containing some caiman, the South American alligators. In the thrillers I read, the baddies seldom escape from their jaws, but these caiman, which were not very big, didn't even blink an eye.

James Hennessy says that, as the only reptile collection in Ireland outside Dublin Zoo, he gets about fourteen thousand visitors a year. In the winter he gives talks to schools, bringing some of his animals along with him. One popular member of this lecture circuit is Rosy, the seven-year-old tarantula who is particularly good-tempered and would love to snuggle up to Miss Muffet. The snapping turtles whose jaws close like mouse-traps, I feel I could find a use for in my life, even as paper clips.

The Reptile Village did have a robbery, when thieves broke in and stole three axolotls. Axolotls are a type of underwater salamander that look like pink sugar mice moulded into shape by a very young child. As soon as the theft was made public, the Reptile Zoo was offered two more. A replacement little pink face peered out at me from its den in an aquarium; though no doubt charming in many ways, I wouldn't have made use of my jemmy and hacksaw in order to possess it.

Extraordinarily enough, there are about one hundred thousand reptiles kept in Ireland and it is causing problems as even a child can buy an 'adorable' little monitor lizard off the Internet and relatively quickly it will have grown to a five-foot monster. James says that he gets an average of four calls a week asking if he would take over these no-longer-wanted pets; amongst them are a worrying number of venomous snakes and crocodiles that can grow up to ten feet long. He is lobbying for legislation on the owning of the more dangerous and possibly invasive reptiles. Many of the North American reptiles can survive the winters here. A Californian Kingsnake was given to him after having been found in a nature reserve in Wexford. It must have either escaped or been let loose. When I met this handsome snake, which did not seem at all indignant at being woken from its winter hibernation, but curled and twisted lovingly round my arm, I was glad to learn that it is non-venomous.

I asked James how his wife Susan likes the reptiles. 'Well, she is not as fanatical about them as I am,' he admits. 'She was keen to get them out of the house so helped a lot with the building of the zoo. At home, we now have only a couple of turtles that belong to the children, a sea eagle owl and two anaconda. They are rather wild so I am getting them used to being handled.'

I imagine them all watching television together, the anacondas wriggling and coiling impatiently round the sofa while watching David Attenborough.

32. *The Overcoat*

The passengers on Friday's 6.20 to Waterford looked like inmates of a morgue, slumped on the seats with pale exhausted faces. The jolly family of Australians who were scattered among us were beings from the real world with their rosy complexions and bright clothes, confident in the knowledge that they had come to find their roots in the land of a hundred thousand welcomes. Any information they winkled out of their fellow travellers they yelled across the carriage to each other: 'Dad, this lady says she's going to Waterford, too.' 'Kyle, wait till you hear this: they have never had such a wet, cold winter before in Ireland.'

A colourless woman in a tweed suit in their midst was doing the crossword. Dad read a clue over her shoulder out loud, because he told us that his daughter Meryln was fair dinkum at puzzles. Meryln thought the answer might be some word that had a double entendre in Australia, which caused huge merriment in the family, and Dad dug the tweedy woman in the ribs so that she would know it was a joke. She clung to her newspaper and filled in another clue. Mum through her giggles said that Dad was wicked and should not shock respectable people so Dad told a comic story, explaining the punchline to the tweedy woman because she did not seem to get it. And he enlightened the rest of the people in the carriage who had given up even pretending to read or sleep. We soon knew all about their Irish roots in Waterford from whence Grandpa had sailed in chains on a convict ship to Botany Bay but had prospered under the Southern Cross; now his descendants had come to visit the ancestral home.

The tweedy woman got up apologetically and clutching her handbag and paper gave a little nod and walked purposefully up the aisle just as the train drew into Carlow. It was after the train had pulled away from the station that Dad saw the tweedy woman's coat neatly folded on the rack. We looked at it aghast – a girl with red hair said that it was the same with her elderly aunt, who was always forgetting things. This crisis bonded the carriage together. No longer did the brashness of the Australians jar on our sensibilities. I wondered if there was any clue as to the identity of the woman in the pockets of the coat and the lady opposite me said that you would not want to be leaving anything around or it would be taken these days. Merylyn, showing more initiative than the rest of us, went in search of the ticket collector. The ticket collector said he would take the coat on to Waterford and it could be claimed back from Lost Luggage. Someone else wondered how she could get off the train on such a cold night and not realize that she had no coat on. The girl with red hair told an anecdote about her aged aunt losing her keys. And Dad, who had studied the timetable, said why not leave the coat in Bagenalstown to be put on the next train back to Carlow. The ticket collector was persuaded to follow this plan and the whole carriage settled back with the virtuous feeling of having done a good turn for someone.

Now, with the ice broken, we were eager to chat to the Australians, to ask them if they knew our relations in Brisbane or Alice Springs, and the red-haired girl told them how she had had a great time working in an abattoir in Melbourne. All too soon there was an announcement over the tannoy that the train was arriving at Kilkenny. The tweedy woman came back down the aisle. The carriage fell silent and then as the implication hit us we hid behind our papers and mobile phones, distancing ourselves as far as possible from the Australians. Not that it was difficult because the Australians had visibly shrunk. The tweedy woman gave her polite little smile and told Dad not to move, because she was getting out at Kilkenny, if he would just pass her coat over.

V

TRAVEL

From Bunnikins to Nagaland

ANNA MUNDOW

The accidental reader, coming across the travel writing of Melosina Lenox-Conyngham (hereafter MLC), enters a booby-trapped landscape. At the outset, the direction seems clear and the going fair. MLC's blithe, inviting sentences seem to say, 'It was a breeze, really; you should have come along.' (Never mind that the journey took hours, or days, in a rattling bus or a floating rust bucket.) Her introductory tone is often – though not always – sedate, almost prim. She informs you of topography, history, weather, architectural heritage and the like. After a decent interval, however, she can no longer hold back. She notices something – and with a single image delivers the first of many delightful shocks.

Describing the romantic Taureg tribesmen of the Malian desert, for example, MLC writes, 'even as we rode camels into the extraordinary silence of the desert, it was broken by a familiar jingle and Mahomet extracted from his long blue robes a mobile telephone that he poked into the folds of his turban'. In the dwelling of a former headhunter in remotest Nagaland, she reports that, 'With hardly a flicker of disappointment at having to turn away from the cricket on the television screen in the corner, he courteously showed us his traditional headdress …' Visiting Imam Ahmed's palace in Taiz, Yemen, preserved in its 1960s glory and filled with clothing and kitsch of the era, she speculates: 'Perhaps instead of being beguiled by Scheherazade, the Imam had a thousand and one reels of Doris Day to watch while his wives were upstairs trying on their Orlon twinsets and patting Lancôme behind their ears.'

Some of us first encountered this eye and wit in conversation and in letters. We prize it now in these essays in the same way that we relish the wink or the raised eyebrow of the irrepressible and irreverent observer. MLC was both. She was also erudite, intellectually shrewd and inventive, as any friend who ever shared with her an adventure, however small, and who later read MLC's written account of the affair, will attest. In a letter dated 2 April 1991, for example, she refers to an overnight visit by an American friend of ours who had never before ventured into the Irish midlands. 'He was so nice,' MLC writes. 'My car has almost lost the perfume it acquired from the pint of cream I poured over the front seat in celebration of his arrival. I hope the faint flavour of the dairy does not still cling to him.' In that small incident, which no one else noticed, she perfectly conveys her panic, his bemusement and the timeless comedy of rural Ireland's encounter with the fastidious American.

The finest of MLC's travel essays have the immediacy of her letters; the astonished sense of at once seeing, and seeing through, a place or a person. Camped on the banks of the river Niger, with an ill-assorted group of companions, she contemplates 'the elderly Hungarian, pulling over his head a pillow case with holes cut for eyes and mouth as he was more fearful of the sun than of any hippopotamus' and an 'American [who] had braved the trip even though a single peanut might send her spinning into eternity'.

In such descriptions, MLC gently satirizes a literary tradition to which she nonetheless belonged, that of the indomitable female traveller. She knew their accounts well, of course, even those of the rather brusque Rosita Forbes who, in the preface to From Red Sea to Blue Nile *(1939), notes that the typical Abyssinian 'carries a parasol and a rifle, but the latter is usually dirty' and that Abyssinians in general are 'very bad shots'. This is not far from MLC's description of her armed guards in Yemen: 'To protect us, they had a mounted machine gun in a pick-up truck. The fact that they wore sandals or open-backed clogs gave one assurance that if an attack took place, they were, at least, not going to run away.'*

But MLC was, thankfully, not steely Rosita Forbes. She did not ride 1100 miles from the Red Sea to the Blue Nile in the 1930s. But had she done so, she would have made light of it, as she so often made light of her remarkable adventures in Africa, India, Asia, Europe, the USA, Eastern and Western Europe and, of course, Ireland. In this respect, her writing carries echoes, above all, of the travel essays of Robert Louis Stevenson. Like Stevenson, MLC often seems to set out on a whim and to welcome whatever and whomever might cross her path. In 'An Inland Voyage', Stevenson, while navigating a Belgian canal, notes that 'Crop-headed children spat on us from the bridges as we went below, with a true conservative feeling.' Admiring the motionless fishermen on the banks, he proclaims, 'I do not care for your stalwart fellows in india-rubber stockings breasting up mountain torrents with a salmon rod …' Similarly, Melo writes of self-regarding explorers who spurn modern synthetic footwear: 'The owners over the years have grown to resemble their boots with leathery tanned skin polished with suncream; gimlet eyes and the tip of the tongue extended in extreme effort.'

Before she could read or write, MLC travelled: as an infant with her mother from wartime Ceylon to South Africa and back again. After that, she never stopped travelling and writing about her travels; those twin activities became the inhalation and exhalation of her literary life. Like her uncle Hubert Butler, however, MLC was also formed as a writer by the fields, woods and riverbanks; the neighbouring farms, small towns and local history of rural Ireland. On such a small stage, each detail is vivid and each encounter potentially rich in drama, at least in the retelling. Everything is noticed. To the great world, MLC brought an eye trained on this modest ground. She also poked fun at her glorious myopia. 'When I travel alone,' she writes, 'the only thing I see is the guidebook and the bus and train timetables – I may have missed the Golden Temple, but I do have an intimate knowledge of Bangkok bus station.'

To read on is to realize that she missed nothing.

33. *The Blue Poppy*

This last summer in the border of a garden in Louth, there was a single blue poppy, the colour as clear as the sky on a perfect spring morning.

These poppies, or to give them their botanical name, *meconopsis speciosa*, were brought to Europe in the early years of the twentieth century by Frank Kingdom-Ward who had found them when looking for plants in south-west China. He had climbed up to about 17,000 feet and was amongst scree on an exposed mountainside when he first saw the poppy: 'I could hardly believe my eyes; surely no flower could be that peerless blue – it must be lumps of turquoise scattered amongst the rocks at the base of the screen.' Scrambling over the stones, he saw that it was really a flower or rather a column of flowers growing on a prickly hollow stem bearing prickly leaves: 'The flowers were of a dazzling azure blue, like Japanese silk in texture and in the centre was a shock of corn yellow stamens.'

A year or so ago, I went to Yunnan, a Chinese province that

borders on Burma and Tibet. It is very remote and known as 'the land beyond the clouds' as there are very steep, high mountains through which three of the great rivers of China flow: the Yangtze, the Mekong and the Salween. Near the Tibetan border, we trekked up from the gorge of the Mekong River among huge, stately pine trees that soared into the mists. They were garlanded with clematis and decorated with long strands of lichen. We climbed up to the pass. At that height, every step was an effort with our lungs gasping for oxygen and our leg muscles pleading for rest. Reaching the top, prayer flags strung across the path in blue, white and yellow flapped in our faces, and we stumbled into the shelter where we crouched round a fire sipping green tea while the porters entertained themselves playing billiards on a real table with a green baize cloth. It seemed particularly bizarre in the roughly built sheds that sheltered us from the rain to which it must have been dragged by mules.

On the other side of the pass, the path zig-zagged through pale-pink and white rhododendrons going steeply down to an idyllic valley surrounded by ragged snow-covered peaks with glaciers, and waterfalls tumbling down into the river below. Under the shade of the trees on the valley floor was a carpet of tiny yellow pansies and wild strawberries. The hedges round the village were of sweet-smelling philadelphus; sprays of dark-red roses clutched at one's clothes; clumps of blue irises grew by the streams and drifts of primulas made patches of colour in the clearing. At twelve thousand feet, this is the indigenous habitat for many plants and shrubs that now flourish in Irish gardens.

After spending the night in one of the large, brilliantly decorated Tibetan houses, I struggled on to the top of the valley through mist and rain. Near the foot of the glacier among the debris of rocks that had broken away from the cliff above was a spark of brilliant blue – a poppy of such perfect blue, it made one gasp.

34. *Dans le Noir*

We did not know what to expect except that it was in the dark. 'Oh well, no need to dress up,' said my niece. We were dining in Dans le Noir, which has lately opened in Barcelona. The address was near the waterfront and in the spacious and well-lit foyer one could have a glass of wine with tapas. By the reception desk was a row of lockers into which we were told to put our coats, bags, scarves and mobile phones, plus anything luminous such as watches or jewellery.

We were then lined up with other patrons in front of a curtained doorway where our waiter, who was called Hector, told us that we should keep our voices low and that if we wanted to leave for any reason, we should call him to guide us out. We then put a hand on the shoulder of the person in front and so in a sort of conga were led by Hector through the door into the dark along a sloping passage – it was eerie because one expected one's eyes to get used to the dark and to be able to make out shapes, and that never happened. Hector parked us in chairs at a table.

I found a knife and fork and a large napkin in front of me. I also found an unknown thigh beside me, but I could not tell if we were all at the same table – there was no way of telling how many people were in the room. It was not only as if I was blind but, owing to not speaking Spanish, I might as well have been deaf.

With extreme caution, I reached out for the glass of wine that was put in front of each of us; it is extraordinary how disorientated one becomes in this solid blackness. We were told later that many people could not tell if it was red or white.

Hector brought us our starter, which was something in sauce – my companions identified it as tofu – and there were pats of pâté and crisps: I knew what they were all right and I found them all over the tablecloth. Was this because of my fumblings with knife and fork? Niece said she had a flower, but I never found one on my plate or perhaps I ate it without registering. Being in the dark should have made my taste buds more acute, but owing to Spanish eating habits that do not consider 10.30 pm late to be dining, I was famished and ready to wolf down everything and more.

The second course, with a different wine, was more identifiable or perhaps that was because the first pangs of hunger were dulled. Anyhow there was duck, there was bacon wrapped round a huge asparagus, some mashed potato and a parsnip croquette with lots of lettuce – I was glad that no one could see me as I was not very good at getting the lettuce into my mouth. Parsimony and weight-watching had combined to make me choose just two courses for our meal.

It was certainly an experience – but it is not something I would like to do too often because not being able to see other diners is so dull. This gave another perspective on the horrors of being blind.

35. Farrera

'The brass bells that hang from the leather collars that the cows all wear ring together like water running over stones, though more musically. There is a blackcap singing on the roof below; a deer gives a rasping cough somewhere on the hillside opposite and two, three, four – no, six magpies swoop past. Otherwise there is silence. No sound of cars, radios, or even of people.'

This is what I wrote in my diary when I was on the annual exchange of artists or writers set up by Annaghmakerrig in Ireland with El Centre d'Art i Natura in the village of Farrera in Spain. A place where artists, poets and musicians can come and work in magical surroundings, undisturbed except for an occasional tractor when the mayor is cutting his hay, or Oppen, the shepherd, is clearing the dung from a shed to tip down into a vegetable garden.

Farrera is in the heart of the Pyrenees in Catalunya, at the head of a valley in the Pallars Sobirà, a small village clinging like ivy to the cliff face. The houses are built back into the rock with the flat, flaky stones of the locality and roofed with heavy rounded slates. On the older houses, the slates have been weathered into a patchwork of different greys, blacks and, where lichen has prevailed, an occasional bright orange. The buildings have been erected higgledy-piggledy up the slope and are connected by steps or paths that pass in and out and even under houses and barns. They are three or four storeys high, but it is often difficult to find the door, which will not be on the level that one expects.

The villages in the Pyrenees have gradually lost most of their population. The hardships suffered during the Civil War and now the difficulties of farming the land economically have caused the original residents to abandon their houses and move to the towns.

In the 1970s and 1980s Farrera attracted newcomers. There was an attempt to set up a commune and though most of the participants went their different ways, they still felt the pull of Farrera. Bernard Loughlin from Belfast came and spent a year with his wife Mary, who had her first child in a house with no electricity or running water. Colm Tóibín was another visitor from Ireland in those early years and Catriona Crowe came to stay for long periods. Bernard and Mary went back to Ireland where he became the first director of the Tyrone Guthrie Centre at Annaghmakerrig, but they spent their holidays in Farrera and eventually bought the semi-ruined Casa Felip. It was in 1989 that he and Jordi Vinas, another member of the original commune who now also owns a house in Farrera, had the idea of the centre and it was eventually set up as a non-profit organization of Farrera Council with funding from various cultural and environmental and government sources. The directors are Lluis Llobet and his wife Cesca Gelabert.

Lluis, a conscientious objector, had worked with the farmers in the mountains instead of doing military service, and had so come to know Farrera. He and Cesca had spent four or five years rebuilding one of the houses and attempting to make a living from sheep. They failed to make sheep pay enough to support the family, so returned to the city where Lluis took a degree in geography and Cesca made pottery. It was Bernard Loughlin who suggested that they should become the first directors of the centre, an inspired choice as the residents testify over and over again in the guestbooks.

The main street of the village passes through the arch under the tower of the little old Romanesque church of St Roc, renovated in the seventeenth century. Though the thirteenth-century altar frontal is in a museum in Barcelona, there is an excellent reproduction in place.

On the far side of the arch is the main plaza, which is an open space with a view across and down the valley to the hills. The centre started in the old school, L'estudi, which had been renovated with European Leader funds. Above the church, up some grass-grown battered steps, is the Casa Ramon where the centre was housed until the Bastion was built. Here, there are available for the artists three studios filled with light, and three comfortable bedrooms whose balconies look out to the hills. There is a kitchen and a well-stocked fridge for snacking or making meals, though every evening the residents gather together either downstairs in the dining room, or, if there are just one or two, in the kitchen of Cesca and Lluis, a room full of warmth, colour and enchantment.

The food! The visitors' book is filled with expressions of delight – one resident upbraids himself for returning again and again to the subject of Cesca's cooking and indeed it is hard not to – delicious salads with grenadines; wonderful fish; and omelettes to die for. When I was there it was autumn, the time to gather wild mushrooms. At weekends, cars would pass by Farrera and go up the barely passable track through the woods, carrying families with huge baskets to fill with *rovellons*, *fredolics*, ceps and other mushrooms. Sometimes I accompanied Cesca or Lala on their mushroom hunts, though most of the ones I found turned out to be poisonous. In spite of my assistance, great baskets full to overflowing were brought home and the next morning Cesca with her cohorts, Lala and Anna, would be seen at a table in the courtyard, cleaning and preparing the mushrooms for our meal that night.

There are strong connections with Ireland and with Annagh-makerrig. Every year two artists exchange for a month. Kerry Hardie came on exchange from Ireland and in her book of poetry, *The Silence Came Close* (2006), there are poems describing Farrera, particularly the view from my window. The writers, poets and artists who come to work here are as diverse as their work. During my month there were a distinguished Israeli short-story writer and his partner, a dramatic performance artist; Rachel Brown the photographer, specializing in pinhole photography, who, though she is an American, spent some years living in Ireland; and a young Egyptian artist on an UNESCO scholarship. He was the only one of us who could work the washing machine.

That month in Farrera with the mountains, the colours and, above all, the silence gave me a personal harmony that I had not known before and I treasure the memory of the little village where, from my balcony, I could spit cherry stones into the chimney of the house below and watch the hill opposite turn a kaleidoscope of autumn colours, which every day became more brilliant as the birches turned to gold and the cherry trees to scarlet.

36. *Les Vélib's*

I pedalled down the Champs-Élysées well in advance of the first posse of the Tour de France. Actually a week ahead, for at that moment Michael Rasmussen and Alberto Contador were battling it out somewhere near the Pyrenees. Back in Paris, on my *vélib'* (which is the nickname for 'free bicycles'), I bicycled, stiff with terror, down the route, for though I was in the special lane reserved for bikes, it is shared with buses and taxis, which I was certain had vengeance in their hearts towards the *vélib's*.

Since the middle of July 2007, 10,648 bicycles at 750 stations have been placed in Paris – and by the end of the year there should be 20,600 bikes at over 1451 locations. These will be within three hundred metres of each other, so it should be convenient to pick up a *vélib'* at one station and return it to another near one's destination.

The *vélib's* are sturdy machines, with three speeds, an easily adjustable seat, a basket, a bell, a chain lock and a self-generating light. And the remarkable fact is that they are not costing the city a penny as they are financed by the international advertising company, JCDecaux, in exchange for sixteen hundred billboards around the city.

There are teething problems; a crowd of hopeful cyclists were gathered at the first station that we went to, where we followed the directions involving credit cards, scanning them this way and that, but the only bicycle that could be released was one with a faulty back tyre. 'Better by taxi!' said my companion, but we persisted. At the next station all the bicycles were in place and the pay screen told us to go elsewhere as there was a fault in the system, so it was at the third station that we got our bikes.

I cannot say I found biking a pleasurable experience as my mind was concentrated on staying upright – they say you never lose the knack, but I am not so sure. Nor can I say I appreciated the beauty of Paris – '*Regardez la vista, c'est magnifique*' – because my eyes were glued to my very immediate surroundings. Only towards the end did I become relaxed enough to realize the ease of this method of travel, which avoids traffic jams and the endless search for a parking place. It is hoped that the bikes will be used by commuters and, to encourage them, the first half-hour is free; after that it is two euro for every hour and a hundred and fifty euro is on deposit from one's credit card in case of the non-return of the bicycle to a station.

This initiative to make Paris a less polluted, greener city is that of left-wing gay mayor, Bertrand Delanoë. Among his other projects has been Paris-Plages, the 2.5-mile-long beach along the Seine where Parisians can toast themselves in the sun, sitting in blue deckchairs on imported sand under palm trees in pots. Another of his schemes has been buying or renting property in the wealthy neighbourhoods and converting it into low-cost accommodation. This has been very contentious as it devalues the property of the middle-class neighbours but, as Delanoë says, they don't vote for him anyway. There is controversy within his ranks, however, because of the huge outlay from the housing budget for relatively few homes.

As we zipped, no, that is hardly a description of my bicycling skills, wobbled, into the Place du Louvre to take an elegant tea under the arcade, I squeaked '*Vive le vélo!*'.

37. *In Aunt Cicely's Footsteps*

'See Amid the Winter Snow' blasted at 5 am through the open window of my hot, very basic room. I released myself from the confines of my mosquito net as the nearby radio continued with half an hour of hymns – which is how the Naga village of Mokochunket wakes to a new day in November.

Though the Naga people at the time were notorious as headhunters, my Aunt Cicely tramped through their hills in the 1920s. This was not so daring as it sounds for she was escorted by an entourage of fifty-five men, which included one man to carry the cook's black cotton umbrella and the kettle. I have to admit my aunt was accompanying the political agent on his official tour of the state. She described how they would start at dawn, when the valleys were filled with mist, and follow the trail through the thick jungle of bamboo, banana and elephant apple twisted with lianas and decorated with orchids, begonias and tree ferns. They traversed ranges of mountains and crossed rivers by bridges made of bamboo that swung wildly when they walked across them.

I was entranced by the thought of this remote place and snatched at the opportunity to go there. This north-east corner of India is politically sensitive as it borders on Burma and in the past has not always maintained a peaceful relationship with the central Indian government. There are some peculiar visa regulations for entering the state. Only parties of at least four or couples that have been 'properly' married may visit Nagaland.

It is an inaccessible region of steep mountain ridges that is inhabited by the Nagas, a unique tribal people whose way of life survived unchanged for five thousand years, and were remarkable for their enthusiasm for headhunting. Alas, we were not as intrepid as Aunt Cicely, whose trek lasted two or three weeks, travelling about two hundred miles. We were picked up by two Land Rovers at the airport at Guwahati in Assam where we had flown from Kolkata.

Our first stop was in Ziro in Arunachal Pradesh where we attended a ceremony for the marriage of an Apatani couple. Women from the village and neighbouring villages came, each carrying a basket suspended from a band across the head. The baskets were filled with the gift of husked rice. In the early morning, with the sun just risen, they walked confidently in a long colourful procession on the narrow bunds that terraced the rice fields.

The baskets of rice were emptied into a granary and then we went on to the feast. I picked fussily at pieces of a piglet that had been sliced up nose to tail and then boiled, bones and all. In spite of my care, I ate a raw chilli that set me skipping in agony to the surprise of my travelling companions who questioned me as to how much rice beer I had drunk, while the feasters, who had downed a lot of rice beer themselves, were delighted at my activity and clutched my hands as we danced in a long line singing a repetitive song.

The Apatanis are known for the beauty of their women, so

much so that neighbouring tribes took to kidnapping the girls for brides. To make the women unattractive, large wooden plugs were put in each side of their noses and their faces were tattooed. I suppose it worked as most of the older women were so disfigured, though the ones under thirty had given up the practice.

The people of Nagaland look far more Burmese than Indian and indeed I crossed a room one day and was in Burma. The houses of the Nagas, particularly the Noctes and the Konyaks, are long palm-thatched sheds on stilts with low walls. In front of each house is an open platform where the gossip takes place and where the women work at their simple looms on which they weave the thick cotton thread into lengths of cloth in the tribal patterns and colours, to be worn as a sarong or a shawl. Headhunting was allegedly practised until 1991, but the skulls that grinned toothily down on us from a shelf looked pretty old and dusty. That might be just because the Nagas have open fires but no chimneys or windows in their houses.

This inaccessible region of steep mountain ridges was a gold mine for anthropologists. There are sixteen major tribes that divide into many sub-tribes, each with their own customs and language. Even during British rule they were only partially administered and were promised self-government on independence. However, the Indian government incorporated the Naga Hills into Assam, which caused the Nagas to conduct a guerrilla war until they were granted a separate state. Though unrest still rumbles on, it is mostly between rival factions of the independence movement.

Traditionally, some tribes are governed on republican principles, others through hereditary chiefs or *anghs*. In one village, an endearing notice read, 'The Chief Angh's residence'. We were made welcome and joined him and the village elders round an open fire on the floor, to admire the display of horns, skins, skulls, spears and shields that hung from the smoke-blackened rafters.

With hardly a flicker of disappointment at having to turn away from the cricket on the television screen in the corner, he courteously showed us his traditional headdress, a skimpy beret of bearskin decorated with the tusks of a wild boar that is tied under the chin. Most of the older men have their faces and bodies tattooed and many of them wear goat horns in the lobes of their ears (useful for carrying tobacco, apparently).

Every village is dominated by a church, if not several: Pentecostal, Revivalist and Roman Catholic sects all have their adherents, but the state is 75 per cent Baptist. One hundred and fifty years ago, American Baptists came to Nagaland and it is now the largest Baptist community in the world, sending missionaries not only to the neighbouring Indian states but much farther afield: our interpreter's brother was a missionary in Zambia. On Sunday, the church I attended in a Konyak village was packed; the choir sang hymns; five gentlemen in specs played guitars; a middle-aged lady said a passionate and extemporary prayer and the congregation listened intently to several lengthy homilies. It is said that in isolated areas the people are returning to their tribal practices and I did see an old belief incorporated into present ritual, for beside the marble tombstone of a wealthy Christian Naga was a half-buried car – for his use in heaven.

In each village there is an imposing building with a soaring thatched palm roof called a *Morung*, which in the past had been the dormitory and meeting place for young men and boys. It was here we saw the collections of human heads. Besides the skulls, the *Morung*s house the ceremonial drum, the hollowed-out tree trunk that the men beat with sticks to make a curious throbbing noise. The wooden pillars in the *Morung*s are carved with animals, particularly tigers, monkeys and snakes, and also carvings of men and women, sometimes of an explicitly sexual nature. The Nagas had very liberal views towards sex before marriage and the men were allowed to visit the unmarried girls.

The few roads in Nagaland are impressive feats of engineering as they wind up and round the steep hills; the annual monsoon often washes away the surface, which makes for a bumpy ride. There was little traffic except for buses and the huge colourful lorries that were decorated with such biblical aphorisms as 'The Lord is the Way' or 'In God we Trust'. The accommodation on this trip varied. There was a tourist hostel in Mopungchuket that had not had many tourists if any – though each little cement cell was carefully numbered and there was one locked room labelled 'conference room'. The village was more concerned for our souls than our comfort; a ghetto blaster was turned on outside our window at 5 am for half an hour of community hymn singing. Another night we stayed in a luxurious bungalow that had belonged to tea planters. It had white pillars, deep verandas, chaises longues and portraits of the ex-owners leading racehorses or photographed with dead tigers.

Kohima, the capital, sprawls over the steep hills. During the Second World War, Japanese troops besieged the town but the Nagas in the surrounding countryside remained loyal. Acting as spies and messengers, they did not offer any support to the Japanese who, with no indigenous assistance, were defeated from the lack of food rather than the heroic defence put up by the Allies. Now there is an immaculate war cemetery with a panoramic view over the countryside.

There is a monument to an earlier battle at the village of Khonoma, where the Nagas had defended themselves successfully against an attack by the British army in 1879. From the memorial at the highest point in this village, we looked down on a lacework of terraced rice fields and across to the hills that protect the Dzukou Valley, which is immortalized by Vikram Seth in his *Beastly Tales from Here and There*.

Decorating the exterior of the houses, clusters of sky-blue orchids or exotic creamy-yellow ones look like hundreds of butterflies gathered together. There are more than three hundred and fifty different species of wild orchid here. Men and women, though mostly women, were returning from working in the fields and the forest. The beautifully woven baskets carried on their backs were filled with heavy loads of grain, firewood or the thick bamboo canes that are used to hold water. They laughed and smiled at us as they wended their way effortlessly up the steep hillside and we, hot and sticky, went back to our Land Rovers.

38. *At Least Mussolini Made the Trains Run on Time*

A girl stormed on to the train muttering to herself in Italian, but when she sat down opposite us, switched to English: 'This train is late again, what can you foreigners think of Sardinia? So backward, no improvements made to the roads or the railways whatever our politicians promise!' The train was ten minutes late, a fact that had been announced on the station board so we had had time to cross the piazza to get a cup of good coffee in a little bar.

Sardinia is very conscious of its infrastructure. In a booklet published by the office of tourism, there is a warning on page one that 'public transport is not without hassles, but can nonetheless hold pleasant surprises as well as unexpected emotions'. The unexpected emotions, one gathers, are mostly fury and frustration, for it explains that one of the railway companies 'proudly' defies electrification and double tracking, which has 'a detrimental effect on the comfort and length of the journey'. The other company, Sardinian Railways, it writes crossly, 'cannot be regarded as a practical means of transport, owing to their un-friendly timetables'.

According to this pessimistic booklet, coach travel is not much better as the island has no motorways so that there is a speed limit of ninety kilometres, which, according to the booklet, 'causes inadequate scheduling, impractical timetables and dis-couraging trip times'.

Guidebooks printed outside the state are more sanguine about the public transport, describing it as 'a reliable way to get around. The main roads are generally good, the traffic light except at the height of summer in tourist centres and Sardinians are the most responsible of Italian drivers.'

Sardinians complain not only about their public transport but also of the taxes that the autonomous regional president, Renato Soru, has introduced for wealthy visitors to the island. They are taxed on their villas and for landing their private planes and, what is infuriating to the very, very rich on the Costa Smeralda, they have to pay a levy to anchor their yachts. Those who own boats over fourteen metres have to pop into a post office to hand over a tax of a thousand euro, while yachts longer than sixty metres will pay fifteen thousand euro. These charges are not paid by Sardinians, but it has them worried that their wealthy tourist trade will go elsewhere and indeed there is a sign up in the port of Bonifacio in nearby French Corsica that reads: 'Merci Monsieur Soru'.

President Soru says that the yacht owners do not spend even one euro in Sardinia and that they can well afford what is known as the luxury tax. He should know, as he is a billionaire, a fortune he made from becoming the first provider on the Continent to offer free Internet access. After the enormous success of this busi-ness, he went into politics and was elected president of Sardinia for the centre left with a personal agenda to protect the envi-ronment of the island and preserve its identity. Immediately after his election, a law was passed banning all building within two kilometres of the coast. Though this enraged the developers, it is generally accepted, as the Sardinians realized that the coast could become another Costa Brava. Less popular is Renato Soru's dislike of mass tourism, which he sees as an exploitation of resources; he wants to shift the emphasis from tourists to real travellers who wish to enjoy a particular experience evocative of Sardinia.

An 'unfriendly' bus timetable stranded us in the town of Nuoro. I can confirm D.H. Lawrence's observation that there is nothing to see there or at any rate not between twelve and five on a Sunday afternoon. However, the pleasure of lying in the shade of a flowering Judas tree eating ice cream was all the experience a bona fide traveller could wish for.

39. *Murder in the Valley*

In Catalunya, north-east Spain, the village of Tor in Vallferrera is set in a deep ravine beside a fast-flowing stream with the mountains towering overhead. The picturesque, tall stone houses with their balconies and shuttered windows are grouped below the small church. Tor has been described as a place of 'cows, horses, perpetual snows' – with an addendum – 'and mafia'. It is the highest settlement in the Pyrenees and to get to it on the Catalan side, there is a rough dirt track leading the ten kilometres from the nearest village. On the other side of the pass above Tor from Andorra there is an asphalt road ending at the border.

Legend has it that Tor was settled by convicts. They and their descendants scratched a living grazing sheep, cattle and horses on the mountainsides. In 1896, the thirteen families of the village signed a legal document that the land should be communally owned by those householders in whose houses 'there was a fire lit all the year round' – in other words, were permanent residents. By 1976, most of the villagers left their homes in the winter to live in more comfortable houses in the valley. But on the other side of the pass, Andorra was booming with duty-free goods and the route through Tor was a highway for smugglers carrying contraband tobacco and alcohol into Spain. Andorra had also become renowned as a centre for skiing and was keen to expand its trails into this valley on the other side of the border.

The last man who still lived more or less permanently in Tor was Sansa. He agreed to a ski station being built on the steep slopes above the village. This was strongly opposed by Palanca ('the Handle'), a buccaneering horse dealer, also a descendant of Tor, who grazed his horses on the mountainside. For twenty years a bitter battle was fought in the courts. Meanwhile, hippies had moved in, some of them working for Palanca and some perhaps acting as bodyguards to the Andorran developer. The struggle continued not only in the courts but also among the bodyguards: two of them were killed. No one was convicted for their murder.

Eventually, the courts reached the decision that Sansa did indeed own the valley. Five weeks later, his body was found, strangled with a piece of electricity cable in his own house. Those arrested for his murder were released without charge and the courts have recently passed judgment that the ownership of the valley now belongs to the heirs of the original thirteen families. Today, the asphalt road from Andorra to the pass above Tor remains an anomaly but, as the whole area has been made a natural park, maybe it will remain so.

It is not only in Tor that the valleys of the Pyrenees are being confronted with change in response to a wealthy society's need for playgrounds, playgrounds that are more for an idle whim or fashion than from necessity. But the agricultural basis for the existence of the small mountain villages such as Tirvia in La Coma is no longer viable. At present most of the old houses are lived in by those whose sons and daughters have migrated to work elsewhere; there is a school, but this year it has only three pupils, and otherwise there is a bakery, a couple of bars and a hostel. Three hundred apartments are being built here that will be used by their owners for perhaps seventeen days a year but will do little to revive the economy of the village. Soon in these valleys there will be no houses behind whose windows a fire is lit throughout the year.

40. The Road to Timbuktu

There are no roads to Timbuktu, that mysterious, remote city of the desert. Trains of camels, laden with slabs of salt, sway slowly through the dunes from the mines that are sixteen days' march to the north. The sand is gradually encroaching; smooth yellow dunes rear up like miniature Alps from the scrubby grey desert around the town. In the streets, the sand is piled up here and there like old snow and at breakfast there is a gritty texture to the bread and to the coffee.

To get here, one can come by four-wheel drive, fly to the very modern little airport that has two flights a week or, as I did, sail down the Niger, the huge river that runs like an artery through Mali northwards towards the Sahara and passes within eight miles of the town. We were transported by an elegant *pinasse*, a slender boat like an elongated canoe with a reed-mat roof to keep off the sun. It was powered by an outboard engine and the trip took three days, camping on the shore at night. There was always something to look at. We passed the small neat villages of the Bozo fishermen; built of mud, they are almost indistinguishable in the landscape but for the groves of mango or eucalyptus trees. Pied kingfishers in their smart lace outfits darted from the bank while blue-bellied rollers like jewels flashed by and herons lazily flew abreast of us. One day, we saw three hippopotami, though not much of them, just three black rims breaking the surface of the water with six sweet little ears.

Mahomet, our guide in Timbuktu, was a Tuareg, the nomadic tribe of the desert and one of the few peoples in the world whose menfolk are veiled. Their heads, mouths and noses are wrapped in five metres of cloth dyed with indigo that often rubs off on their skin so that they are also called the 'blue people'. But even as we rode camels into the extraordinary silence of the desert, it was broken by a familiar jingle and Mahomet extracted from his long blue robes a mobile telephone that he poked into the folds of his turban.

Timbuktu – the name alone has a fascination for the traveller. Two hundred years ago it cast such a spell that the French Geographical Society offered two thousand francs for the first European to reach it and return alive. Gordon Laing, who had been attacked and badly wounded en route, did get to the city but was murdered there, so it was a Frenchman, René Caillié, disguised as a Muslim trader, who reached the fabled city and returned to France to claim the prize.

Travellers who reach Timbuktu are often disappointed by the city itself; even René Caillié wrote that it was 'nothing but a mass of ill-looking houses built of earth'. Gone are the great universities and libraries that made it so famous in the past. Now, as in Caillié's day, it is a sprawl of dusty, mud-built, flat-roofed houses and narrow lanes. Only in the cool darkness of the mosque, which has no decoration but a forest of pillars, does one get a sense of the history of this once-great trading place for gold, ivory, slaves and salt. The nomadic Tuareg still come with their

salt-laden camel trains, though nowadays they are also quite keen
to carry off the tourists to take tea in their nearby camps. Sadly,
as it was Ramadan I never did see how our Tuareg host managed
to sip from the communal glass of foaming sweet tea through
the five metres of indigo-dyed cloth swathed around his head
and face.

There is much more to see in Mali, this huge landlocked
country in West Africa, than sand, camels and hippopotami. To
the south of Timbuktu, the town of Djenné rises above the sandy
plain like an island. When the rains have been good it is indeed
an island as the dry, encircling riverbed is filled with water. A
dramatic and magnificent mosque, the largest mud-built struc-
ture in the world, dominates the city. A photographer's dream,
especially when the weekly market is taking place in the square
in front of the mosque. Then there is a kaleidoscope of colour:
women in brilliantly patterned long, cotton dresses with match-
ing turbans, Bozo men in blue gowns and conical hats, Tuaregs
with only their long eyelashes curling between the folds of their
turbans and all kinds of merchandise from peanuts to fresh fish
(rapidly getting less fresh), jewellery, calabashes, sacks of millet,
fruit and vegetables. There were lengths of dress material gaily
printed with the picture of the president or, like one I saw, with
a jolly design of computers. The most picturesque moment is
in the late afternoon when the women pile into carts drawn by
oxen, horses or a troika of donkeys, and make their way home
across the sands to their villages.

The town itself is a collection of narrow, twisted alleyways
between tall, Moroccan-style houses dating from the fifteenth
century when Djenné was a rich trading city. The walls of the
houses are made of dried-mud bricks, and then plastered with
mud, which makes them look as if they have been constructed of
elephant skin. The heavy wooden doors are elaborately pierced
and decorated. Inside there is a courtyard where there are sheep,

goats, donkeys and children; women stand with a heavy cudgel that they thump down into a wooden container of millet, crushing it into flour; this thudding is perhaps the most evocative sound of the Malian villages.

The most remarkable site in Mali is the spectacular Bandiagara Escarpment that extends for one hundred and fifty kilometres and is inhabited by the Dogon people. Centuries ago the Dogons built their villages clinging to the cliff face. They are made of mud with strange little granaries that look like sentry boxes with conical thatched roofs. The small doors in these buildings are elaborately carved with figures and symbols of the animist gods on which the Dogon culture and lifestyle is based. One comes on fetishes or sacred objects in unexpected places. In every village there is a thickly thatched roof propped up on nine ornately carved pillars, which is where the elders gather to discuss the affairs of the village. It is only about four feet high so that if anyone gets too angry they hit their head when they jump up to protest (what about that as an idea for Dáil Éireann!).

We trekked along and down the escarpment for three days across the bare rock, scrambling into ravines where there were brilliant green patches of onions, which the Dogons cultivate assiduously, and high up on the inaccessible precipices, where one finds the tombs of the Telli people who preceded the Dogons. We clambered down clefts in the rock to the Dogon villages at the base of the cliff. Most of them have *campements*: enclosed courtyards where visitors can have their meals and sleep on the surrounding flat roofs – after climbing a very primitive ladder, I say with feeling! But once up, one lies under the sparkling stars listening to the chatter of the village echoing strangely off the cliff face. When that grows quiet, there are the donkeys, the dogs and, most noisy of all, the cocks that herald the dawn many hours before the sun comes up, and there is the call by muezzin to prayer before sunrise. But hiking up and down the cliff face, following the ancient paths that twist up the fissures in the rock or down into gulches, soon cures any sleeping problems at night.

Mali is not for the sun lover, as much time is spent trying to avoid it by starting very early in the morning and snoozing in the shade during the midday hours. Nor would it attract the gourmet, though the Nile perch or *capitaine*, as it is known locally, was delicious and widely available. There was any amount of fruit and most meals were based on couscous or sweet potatoes. But for the adventurous it is one of the most fascinating and unspoilt countries to visit.

41. *Williamsburg*

I was met at the bus station in Williamsburg by Cousin Bryan, who looked as if he had stepped from the pages of *Mother Goose's Nursery Rhymes* as he was wearing knee breeches, white stockings, a tricorn hat and had silver buckles on his shoes. Out on the street, however, his appearance was unremarkable, as stout matrons and young girls in mob caps and print gowns bustled by on the sidewalks. It was I, in my jeans, who looked out of place, or rather time.

Cousin Bryan was on an exchange programme to the College of William and Mary at Williamsburg. Williamsburg had been the chief city of the British colony until the American Revolution. In spite of having been burnt by the revolutionaries, it still retained some of the old red-brick buildings of the settlers and in the 1930s, with the help of Rockefeller money, the city was tidied up and houses rebuilt so that Williamsburg is now much more appealing and authentic than it could have ever looked during its golden age. To add more charm and encourage sightseers to shop,

shop, shop, the sales staff in the main street wear eighteenth-century dress.

Bryan looked at his watch that he pulled on a chain from some recess in his clothing, and said we must hurry as he was on duty in ten minutes. We raced off to Ye Olde Bakery into which Bryan vanished and emerged, holding a steaming tray of buns that gave forth the delicious aroma of new bread. Bryan balanced the tray at a perilous angle on one upraised hand above his head while with the other he rang a bell and ran down the street crying out: 'Hot cross buns, hot cross buns, one a penny, two a penny, hot cross buns!' The tourists and I, snuffling like hounds scenting a fox, followed the delicious aroma to Ye Olde Pastry Shoppe where we found hot cross buns laid out ready to be purchased, though for rather more than a penny.

I thought that possibly Bryan might give me one of his wares so looked behind the curtain to find his tray propped up against the wall with the buns still on it. 'Oh, they are glued on and sprayed to make them smell of new bread; the dry ice makes them look as if they are fresh out of the oven,' he told me.

On his arrival in Virginia, Cousin Bryan had found himself much in demand as an English officer for the re-enactments that were performed of various battles of the American Revolution. His promotion was meteoric; he joined as a common foot soldier but had risen to be the general in charge of the British forces within half an hour and thought he might get curvature of the spine from all the medals he had to wear. The pinnacle of his military career was at the re-enactment of the Battle of Yorktown, which had been a singular defeat for the British. The numbers on the rebellious American side were inflated by the descendants of the original fighters, who included the Daughters of the American Revolution. Some of these ladies donned the uniform of their male ancestors and others acted as camp followers in elegant gowns with fichues.

The whole charade was taken extremely seriously and the revolutionaries spent a long time posing for the cameras of the local papers when they had to explain exactly who they were and what their relationship was to the original rebels. Nobody was interested in the ancestry of those on the English side, who were dressed in uniforms with broad white straps crossing from either shoulder and tall hats like high tea cosies on their heads or were done up as Indians (the English had difficulty in recruiting from the patriotic students, but as historically some Indians had sided with the loyalists, it was considered less ignoble to appear in the part as a redskin).

They were ready for war long before their adversaries and while they were hanging around, Bryan saw that this was an opportunity to redress the balance of history. He devised a dexterous flanking movement, which engaged the main body of his troops, leaving only a few to man the reproduction cannons from which blanks only could be fired. The plan of attack succeeded brilliantly, catching the enemy completely by surprise. Bryan had appeared out of the bushes accompanied by a lot of Indians in full warpaint. With whoops and howls and some skilful manoeuvres by Bryan and his officers, they overpowered the American forces, though they had more difficulty with the Daughters of the American Revolution who put up heavyweight and spirited resistance, in spite of being hampered by their hooped skirts. The loyalists ran up the Union Jack on every flagpole. There was an unfortunate episode when General Washington was scalped by an Indian brave, or at least his wig was snatched from his head and borne round the battlefield on the point of a halberdier, with the Indians singing the college football song and doing a war dance in a procession behind it, before it was consigned to the flames of a fire of hot coals that had already been lit in preparation for the evening's barbecue.

A television camera crew filmed the battle throughout. It

was rumoured that the director was cavorting with his mistress, leaving the cameramen to do their work, and he did not take in the changed circumstances of the historic battle so let it go out as part of the news that night. The American public was astonished to learn that it was still a British colony.

There was an enquiry afterwards and the victory was put down to the revisionism of modern historians. General Washington made an indignant complaint about his treatment or rather the treatment to his wig. Bryan admitted that he had allowed the British army to consume the very generous rum ration before battle commenced, which, as he pointed out, would have been the case in the real combat, but he was stripped of his medals and dismissed from the service, hence his employment in the Pastry Shoppe.

Bryan and I wandered about Williamsburg, skipping out of the way of sedan chairs and being hit by the enormous baskets that the matrons of the town carried. There was a lot of bowing and curtseying and adding an 'e' on to words: 'Ye are welcome to this humble confiture shoppe', or 'What kind of fare does Dame Conyngham wish to partake of for her luncheon from our selection of jellabubs and syllabubs?'

It was a steppe forward in tyme to return to the bus station and buy a ticket from the grumpy lady who snarled, 'Wareyrsayyr wannato go?' and 'Ain't you got the right change?' So with the lace-edged handkerchief I had bought as a souvenir I waved farewell to Williamsburg and took the Greyhound bus to Charlottesville.

42. The Land of the Queen of Sheba

And when the Queen of Sheba heard of the fame of Solomon concerning the name of the Lord, she came to prove him with hard questions. And she came to Jerusalem with a very great train, with camels that bear spices, and very much gold, and precious stones.

1 Kings 10

Solomon skilfully answered her interrogation and so impressed her with his great wisdom that, as we are told in 1 Kings 10: 'She gave the king an hundred and twenty talents of gold, and of spices very great store, and precious stones. There came no more such abundance of spices as these which the Queen of Sheba gave to King Solomon.'

From the Koran we know that King Solomon had first heard of the fabulous kingdom of Sheba and its queen from his magical bird, a hoopoe that often whispered bits of news into his ear. After they had exchanged letters she travelled to meet him. The encounter, one might say, has received much media attention and the gossip columnists of the day put it about that Solomon manoeuvred her into showing her hairy legs and her foot like a donkey's hoof by making her walk across a mirrored floor, and that he inveigled her into his bed. This liaison is said to have resulted in a son, Menelik, who, though brought up by his mother, visited his father who introduced him to the Jewish faith and dispatched him to Ethiopia. The Emperor Haile Selassie the 225th and last monarch claimed direct descent from Menelik.

'And King Solomon gave unto the Queen of Sheba all her desire, whatsoever she asked, beside that which Solomon gave her of his royal bounty. So she turned and went to her own country, she and her servants.' Her kingdom of Sheba or Saba was in south-west Arabia in what is now Yemen and centred round Marib at the edge of the desert known as the Empty Quarter. The wealth of the country came from its control of the incense route. Three thousand years ago, the caravans of camels padded from the coast in the south through Marib on their way to Mecca and Syria. They were loaded with spices from India, Somalia and Zanzibar, but their most valuable merchandise was frankincense. This is an aromatic gum that is milked from the ugly *Boswellia sacra* trees, forests of which once grew in the gullies of the great wadis in the Hadhramaut.

Foreigners were under the misapprehension that it was so precious that the groves of incense trees were protected by deadly flying serpents that could only be pacified by the smoke of a rare shrub. Incense was a much sought-after and prized commodity: Egyptians used it with another Arabian product, myrrh, to perfume and preserve the dead for the afterlife; Herodotus tells us that frankincense was used by Assyrian ladies before they made love; and it was burnt on all the altars to the gods of the Eastern Mediterranean. Jerusalem imported one hundred and fifty-nine jars of frankincense in one year, Chaldean priests burnt ten thousand talent-weight annually on the altar of Bel in Babylon and, after capturing Gaza, Alexander the Great, whose tutor had once criticized him for his extravagant use of incense in the temple, sent the man five hundred talents of incense with the message that 'there was no longer any need to be parsimonious to the Gods'. The biggest market was Rome where Pliny wrote about funerals in which heaps of odours were piled up in honour of the bodies of the dead, saying that incense 'is the luxury of man, which is displayed even in the paraphernalia of death, thus has Arabia been rendered "happy" '.

The rules for the caravans were strict: there was no deviating from the road on pain of death to the carriers, and they had to pay high taxes to all the cities they passed through as well as the cost of feeding and water. The trade route was as valuable as oil is to a country in the present day. With the idea of expanding their empire, the Romans sent an army under Aelius Gallus to capture the wealth of Arabia, but when they were within two days of Marib, 'the land of incense', they had to turn back for lack of water.

It is said that one could travel in continuous shade for two months through the lands of Marib. But now the dusty plain with just a few scratchings of cultivation stretches between the mountains and the desert. Seven hundred years before Christ, a dam was built across the narrow part of a wadi. The barrage wall or dyke, which was made of rough stones with sand and mud, has gone, but the huge sluice gates that controlled the water for two canals were built of cut-stone blocks slotted together with pegs and they are as impressive as they ever were. Still discernible are the remains of the old irrigation system that distributed the water to a plain so fertile that it yielded two crops a year and made Marib famous throughout the Middle East. But there was always a problem with silt deposits and every two hundred years or so the wall of the dam had to be raised and when this was neglected it eventually collapsed around 570 AD.

The dam was reckoned by Muslims to be one of the wonders of the world and its destruction is referred to in many poems and stories. One version says a rat came to Marib from Syria by jumping from hump to hump along an immense caravan of camels and on reaching the dam took to digging holes in the dyke with its paws and moved a huge boulder with its hind legs that fifty men could not have rolled from its place. A soothsayer did not need a great deal of acumen to point out to the king that a calamity was about to occur and the land laid waste.

The king, with all the wiliness of a modern property dealer, invited the chief men of the city to a splendid feast that, in accordance with a preconceived plan, was interrupted by a violent altercation between himself and his son. Blows were exchanged and the king cried out, 'O, shame on the day of my glory, a stripling has insulted me and struck my face.' He swore that he would put his son to death, but the guests entreated him to show mercy, until at last he gave way. 'But by God,' he exclaimed, 'I will no longer remain in a city where I have suffered this indignity. I will sell my lands and my stock.' He sold off his kingdom to the speculators for as much gold in coins as would reach the hilt of his sword when he stuck it in the ground, and hastily departed. The dam burst, spreading devastation far and wide and drowning among others 'a thousand beardless youths upon a thousand skewbald horses'.

Asha, one of the most famous of the Arabian poets, wrote of the dam:

> It watered their acres and vineyards, and hour
> By hour, did a portion among them divide.
> So lived they in fortune and plenty until
> Therefrom turned away by a ravaging tide.
> Then wandered their princes and noblemen through
> Mirage-shrouded deserts that baffle the guide.

The Sabean people from Marib scattered and emigrated, but after fifteen hundred years the Sheik of Abu Dhabi, who traces his ancestry back to those who fled with the king before the disaster, has built a new dam farther back in the hills, which one day perhaps will bring greenery and prosperity back to Marib.

A few miles away there is a sign for Bilquis's palace. Bilquis is the name of the Queen of Sheba. The palace – possibly a temple to the moon – has four slender columns standing in the sand and there are walls and steps leading to a marble altar. An excavation was interrupted by tribal hostility many years ago and the desert is creeping back, for even as we looked at it a sand storm blew up around us, making the air gritty and obscuring the pillars from our view.

The old town of Marib is built on a small hill – it looks most romantic with tall, mud tower houses growing out of the earth and it is not until one gets near that one realizes the town is in ruins. Most of the towers have cracks in them or have half-fallen away; others have collapsed altogether and their mud bricks are melting back into the earth from whence they came. In this remote and desolate region, one is not surprised that a mediaeval city should fall into ruin; the destruction, however, is not the result of time, but for the more contemporary reason that the town was bombed. It was a royalist stronghold during the civil war in the 1960s and the Egyptians, allied with the republican government, blitzed the place. Now only a few families live in the dusty, rather eerie towers. Children took us into their house, up the stairs past rooms with no furniture in them, just heaps of rags and sticks. The guide called for the woman of the house, but no one answered and we stood in the shuttered room, embarrassed at the way we had pushed in uninvited. There was a little rustle from a dark corner and we realized it was the woman crouching there so that she could not be seen unveiled by the men of the party. When they left, she came out quite merrily and asked for baksheesh. On the fifth floor was a kitchen with an open fire and blackened walls and we climbed out on the flat roof looking over at the mountains. Below us at the foot of the hill was the crumbling mosque with its forty-two columns that supported the now sagging roof. Some of the columns are carved in such a way that they must have been taken from an ancient Sabean temple. In the dusty paths that did as streets, donkeys brayed and children crowded about us asking for biros. An Arab poet wrote:

Himyar and its kings are dead, destroyed by Time:
Duran by the Great Leveller laid waste.
Around its courts the wolves and foxes howl,
And owls dwell there as though it never was.

Our guards, for we had been given an armed guard in case the tribesmen took it into their heads to kidnap us, looked bored. Their bright, cotton, camouflage uniforms of blue and brown, giraffe-like yellow and brown or even a fetching pink and red, showed up cheerily against the arid background. To protect us, they had a mounted machine gun in a pick-up truck. The fact that they wore sandals or open-backed clogs gave one the assurance that if an attack took place, they were, at least, not going to run away. But when we turned on to the road for Sanaa, the capital of Yemen, they accelerated past us – perhaps to clear the way ahead or perhaps to race for home and safety.

Some say that Sanaa is the oldest inhabited city in the world, having been founded by Shem, the eldest son of Noah who, as the waters went down, hopped off the ark onto a high plateau and started to lay out the town, until a large bird snatched his measuring tape up in its beak and dropped it on the other side of the plateau under a steep, rocky mountain. Shem, taking this for an omen, moved to the new site. Up to the 1960s, the city was still walled and the gates were shut at night. Since then the suburbs have rampaged over the plain, but have left the centre almost untouched.

Two thousand years ago, Sanaa was dominated by the great

palace of Ghumdan. It has been much acclaimed by poets and historians who describe it as a huge edifice of twenty storeys. At each corner stood a brazen lion and when the wind blew it entered the hollow interior of the effigies and made a sound like roaring lions. The roof was a slab of pellucid marble so that when the Lord of Ghumdan lay on his couch he saw birds fly overhead and could distinguish a raven from a kite.

If Paradise's garden is above the skies,
Then hard by heaven the roof of Ghumdan lies.
And if God made on Earth a heaven for our eyes,
Then Ghumdan's place is by that earthly paradise.

The palace of Ghumdan may be only a mound of earth now, but the houses of Sanaa are beautiful. Each one is a small square tower going up sometimes as high as nine storeys; the smooth mud exterior is embellished with designs of white plaster like icing on gingerbread. There are panes of either coloured glass or alabaster set in fanlights above the shuttered windows to allow in the light. The most elaborately decorated interior is the single room on the top floor with windows opening over the city and cushions round the walls. This is where guests are welcomed and this is where the men gather to chew *qat*, a mild narcotic that 'dispels grief and anxiety'. Yemenis are addicted to the drug and it bulges like a tennis ball in one cheek. There is a whole economy based on *qat*, and in the countryside little terraced fields of *qat* bushes are guarded by individual stone towers.

Sanaa has a labyrinth of narrow streets and alleys that twist and turn, come unexpectedly into little squares or on mosques and wiggle into the *suq*. This is the market in which each street has a different speciality: a *suq* of tinsmiths with their wares dangling from strings around the doorway; a raisin *suq*; the *suq* of the *janbiya*, the curved dagger worn in the middle of the stomach; a *suq* for henna where, peering through an open door, one can see in the dark interior a blindfolded camel turning a wheel for the grinding of sesame oil. All is brilliant colour and movement, punctuated by the women wrapped in black, with only the eyes showing, and sometimes even they have a black veil covering them.

Thomas Moore in *Lalla Rookh* took it on himself to describe 'the fresh nymphs bounding o'er Yemen's mounts', but we did not see much sign of them. The women that we saw in the countryside were carrying great trusses of the maize stalks that are used for fodder on their heads, or labouring under bundles of thorny twigs for firing, or bringing buckets of water from the well.

Away from Sanaa, the villages and small towns have stone or mud-built tower houses with highly embellished exteriors and thick, wooden old doors that have been ornately decorated. The towns nestle beneath a defensible position or perch on craggy eminences. It is easy to imagine the *jinns* from the *Arabian Nights* living in these mountain fastnesses and the phoenix, that fabulous bird, laying itself to die on a fire of cinnamon and sprigs of incense to rise again from the ashes.

Looking down on Wadi Dhahr from the steep red cliffs above is like looking down on an oasis, so green and fertile does the valley floor appear. There are orchards of pomegranates, peaches and apricots; vineyards and walled gardens. In the middle is the extraordinary palace, Dar al-Hajar, built by the Imam Yahya in the 1930s. It is one of the most photogenically spectacular buildings in the world. Perched on a rock as if about to catapult into space at any moment, it is elegantly decorated on the outside, but cool and empty inside.

In contrast, the last Imam's palace in Taiz has been left as it was in 1962 when Imam Ahmad died. The foyer is hung with photographs of public executions of dissidents, including two of the Imam's brothers. They were both beheaded but were given a splendid banquet beforehand. In the other rooms, it is as if Dickens's Miss Havisham was having a jumble sale; there are rails and cupboards of clothes, hundreds of heavily embroidered silk coats, twenty-three waistcoats, nylon blouses, cardigans, strapless bras, vases of plastic roses, picnic flasks, together with tins of Twinings Earl Grey tea. The Imam's medicines, bandages and wheelchair are on display: in the last year of his life, in an attempted assassination, three army officers emptied their revolvers into him at point-blank range then turned him over to check that he was dead before they fled. But the Imam, who had always claimed that he was impervious to bullets, survived, albeit in a precarious state of health.

In a state room there is gold furniture and a dusty gold throne, a cuckoo clock hangs on the wall, Revlon suitcases, pressure cookers and electric beaters are piled on tables. Cobwebs dim the Venetian chandeliers. On the fourth storey is a sitting room with a suite of pink sofas and chairs; a standard lamp with a fringed shade stands in a corner and, on a table by the window, a long-playing gramophone. There are Bakelite radios, cigarette boxes from Japan, hundreds of fountain pens; a collection of stamps, jewels displayed in old-fashioned glass cases and a whole room devoted to perfumes: family-sized bottles of Christian Dior and Guerlain jostle on the crowded shelves with shampoo and Old Spice. There is a room with a projector so that the Imam could have his private cinema. Perhaps instead of being beguiled by Scheherazade, the Imam had a thousand and one reels of Doris Day to watch while his wives were upstairs trying on their Orlon twinsets and patting Lancôme behind their ears.

But now the Imams have been swept away; the kings and queens have long gone. One can reflect with Omar Khayyám:

Think, in this batter'd Caravanserai
Whose Doorways are alternate Night and Day,
How Sultan after Sultan with his Pomp
Abode his Hour or two, and went his way.

Alas, the caravanserai has become more than battered – it has become a petrol station – but still the ghost of camel bells can be heard heralding the arrival of the Queen of Sheba.

43. *Carbon Footprint*

In the grey dawn I could hear a hippopotamus stumbling through our camp. Realizing the dangers if he turned nasty, I put my hand under my pillow – not for my trusty revolver but for my false teeth. There is nothing that gives a girl confidence like having a full set of gnashers in place.

My intrepid companions under canvas on the banks of the Niger were also arming themselves. I could hear them searching for their glasses, their walking sticks or, in the case of the elderly Hungarian, pulling over his head a pillow case with holes cut for eyes and mouth as he was more fearful of the sun than of any hippopotamus. One might think it strange to make the journey through the desert to Timbuktu if even a sunbeam was likely to kill you, but of our small party of seven, he was not the only one with a life-threatening allergy. One American had braved the trip even though a single peanut might send her spinning into eternity. As peanuts are one of the staple foods of Mali, this was indeed to dice with death. Therefore hippopotamuses came pretty low on the list of perils for our group and indeed this one plodded into the river and sank beneath the waves, so all we could see were two sweet little ears as we hobbled out of our tents to face the day.

Those who are attracted by travel companies that advertise safaris or treks that 'venture' rather than drive consider themselves a tough breed. They prefer not to go it alone for various reasons including the convenience of having the arrangements made for them and then the pleasure of complaining about them. When I travel alone, the only thing I see is the guidebook and the bus and train timetables – I may have missed the Golden Temple, but I do have an intimate knowledge of Bangkok bus station and the facilities there or lack of them.

However, we are no softies. 'Oh no, we would never have a beach holiday, that is not our scene at all. Though if you do want to spend time by the sea, there are the most divine beaches round Trincomalee, little coves of golden sand and absolutely no one else there ... Well, yes, I expect there were a few Tamil Tigers lurking in the jungle and Rodney did stand on a stingray but he was quite all right after a few days in hospital.'

The word 'tourist' must never be mentioned except as a derogatory term for crowds of sun-pink people, in inappropriate shoes, who clog the view of the Acropolis or other wonders of the world. Participants in 'activity adventures' have usually travelled extensively: they have caught fleas in Quetta and taimen (giant trout) under a full moon in Mongolia and have many, many, many amusing tales to share round the campfire.

'... the pilot lost his way so landed in a dried-up riverbed. It was forty degrees centigrade, but nobody was allowed to leave the plane because we had not cleared customs ...'.

'... thirty-seven hours hidden under a tarpaulin in the back of a truck to get to Lhasa ...'.

'... so I took a taxi to the Black Desert ...'.

After a couple of days, these anecdotes pall on listeners who have themselves been there and done that, and the talk turns to more homely subjects. In China, after we had trudged up to a pass in the Kawa Karpo range, we sat drinking green tea looking down through gigantic pine trees wreathed in clematis to the Mekong River. Everyone had much to say about Aga cookers; the Cramptons had a four-door Aga, while the Bowens had only a two-door Aga and the Hasselbads, being American, had no Aga at all. This enthralling subject kept everyone happy as we slid through mud and down precipices to the valley below.

On these tours there is no question of marching on one's stomach, we are all wearing boots – 'I have had this pair for twenty years and they have never let me down – leather, of course, which makes them heavier than the modern synthetic ones, but they can breathe.' The owners over the years have grown to resemble their boots, with leathery tanned skin polished with suncream; gimlet eyes and the tip of the tongue extended in extreme effort.

Suitcases and bags are battered and rubbed, wheels are regarded with suspicion, but canvas knapsacks, new in the day of Baden-Powell, are much admired. Packed among the hand-knitted socks and woolly vests is always a garment suitable in case an invitation is extended by a provincial governor or the ambassador, 'who is the second cousin of the son-in-law of my neighbour, Maisy Callaghan'.

On the trip to China, the instincts that made the Empire great surfaced at traumatic moments. 'What time is dinner?' asked a gentleman from Gloucestershire as we bounced along a barely discernible track that bisected a precipice. The driver was peering anxiously ahead for any pebble rolling off the cliffside that might indicate a landslide. Several times we had had to stop and clear the road of huge boulders that had come down a very short time before. The wife of the man from Gloucestershire appeared not to have noticed anything untoward and was instructing the

Chinese courier on the intricacies of the British peerage. The courier, who knew that the driver had taken the wrong turning some way back but did not like to lose face by telling us that we were lost, repeated in bemused tones: 'A baron is called a lord and has an honourable son and a ladylike wife.' He had not yet mastered the English R.

We did survive, but that night I was truly grateful for our 'drinkie poos'. This ceremony took place before 'dinner' when one was invited by a member of the party to partake of a slug of Scotch from a tooth mug in their room or tent while one criticized the way the tour was being organized, or those members of the party who have not been invited to 'drinkie poos'.

After returning home, there are only the photographs to remind me of where I have been and what I have seen and those who shared these experiences with me. 'Such a good snap of you attempting to eat noodles, I know you would like to have it.' Or: 'Harry standing on his head in that bar in Timbuktu, wasn't it a hoot!' There are so many pictures that they block my email and I am unable to press the delete button.

VI

PERSONAL

Dropping Frozen from the Bough

SOPHIA GRENE

It was always hard to feel sorry for Melo because she projected such an air of self-sufficiency, and told such funny stories about her trials and mishaps. It is clear from reading these pieces, some of them very personal, that, like the bird in D.H. Lawrence's poem 'Self Pity', dropping 'frozen dead from the bough', she did not waste time feeling sorry for herself. But neither did she have a Panglossian view, sweeping problems under the carpet, transforming them instead into comic or dramatic anecdotes.

It would have been very difficult to feel sorry for Auntie, as she liked to style herself. I don't think the concept ever crossed my mind, certainly not until she became ill. Even when she was very ill and we were all worried for her, pity was never part of the mix. In many ways, Melo had an enviable life, but much of it was down to what she made of it. Some people might find the single life, particularly living alone, difficult, but Melo gave the impression of relishing it, and it is hard to imagine her compromising her individuality enough to share her home.

I think of her often when I read Emma Woodhouse's predictions for her own future as an unmarried woman. 'Mine is an active, busy mind, with a great many independent resources; and I do not perceive why I should be more in want of employment at forty or fifty than one-and-twenty,' she remarks to her friend Harriet, who is appalled at the thought of becoming an old maid.

> *And as for objects of interest, objects for the affections, which is in truth the great point of inferiority, the want of which is really the great evil to be avoided in not marrying, I shall be very well off, with all the children of a sister I love so much, to care about. There will be enough of them, in all probability, to supply every sort of sensation that declining life can need. There will be enough for every hope and every fear; and though my attachment to none can equal that of a parent, it suits my ideas of comfort better than what is warmer and blinder. My nephews and nieces! – I shall often have a niece with me.*

Melo tended to treat her nieces as enhanced pets, to be called on when they might provide amusement or an opportunity for didactic entertainment, but, speaking as one of the nieces who served such a useful purpose, it was always an unpredictable and exciting pleasure to be called upon. Working in London, one might receive a phone call out of the blue: 'Hello, it's your Auntie here, can I take you to tea in the British Museum?' The venue was chosen, it turned out, because of its Malian exhibits, which Melo wanted to inspect ahead of her trip to Timbuktu. One rarely had prior warning of these events, but it always seemed worth dropping daily business to find out what was planned this time.

In some ways, Melo's life seemed very public – she turned it into a sort of performance and most of all a source of stories – but she never gave much away about her interior life. As a result, some of these later pieces seem too personal for comfort – reading them is like reading her diary. But, after all, Melo made a career out of reading other people's diaries, so perhaps we may be forgiven.

44. *A Lovesome Thing*

Alas, nobody but myself appreciates my horticultural skills. In early summer I spend much time at my window admiring the garden, or rather the very small plot in front of my wee cot. Then it is a vivid carpet of flowers, scarlet poppies, yellow-eyed daisies and lacy cow parsley. Dandelions star the ground, making it resemble the sky on a frosty night, and sweet rocket, with its clouds of white and pale-mauve spikes of blossom, perfumes the air more exotically than roses; the soapwort, which, against everyone's advice, I imported from a ditch in Wicklow because of its scented flowers in autumn, is now surging round my garden with the speed of an express train, but I do not think it will take over because the convolvulus or bindweed is fighting back. Someone once said that they could not think why the whole world is not bound and strangled by bindweed and this question preoccupies me to such an extent that I lean on my spade and ponder like Archimedes on his pillar, during which time it has been able to tie up a gooseberry bush and strangle the foxgloves that were to be such a feature.

At this season, when the soapwort and bindweed are only indulging in trench warfare and have not yet got round to hand-to-hand fighting, my garden is not only filled with colour but it also promises healthy, economical and labour-free food. There is lamb's lettuce, which looks like an anaemic forget-me-not. It can be used at a pinch or rather with a large pinch of herbs as a salad; likewise dandelion leaves. When I was in France, the family I boarded with screamed with what I took to be pleasure the day this delicacy appeared on the menu. After having eaten the salad I realized that it was screams of admiration for another of Madame's cost-cutting ideas.

Nettles are keen contenders for space in my landscape: the books inform me that when young they make an 'appetising' vegetable and a delicious soup. Every year with much pain I gather the nettle tops and though no doubt I am bouncing about filled with vitamin C and iron, it is like eating old mackintoshes. I end up by describing my prolific nettles as 'my butterfly garden', though both I and the caterpillars would infinitely prefer a row of cabbages. The most prevalent shrub that surrounds me is the elder, which is covered with creamy plates of blossoms in the early summer. When picked they smell like tomcats but if one perseveres they can be made into the most delicious cordial. Elder is traditionally supposed to have been used for the wood of the Cross and was also the tree from which Judas Iscariot hanged himself. It certainly has witchy qualities. Like Birnham Wood, my elders are on the move, and like Macbeth I fear they are closing in on me.

The calendar of my garden is always the same: the year starts with optimism about nature's bounty, but by mid-summer I have to admit a serious error in my philosophy and that my garden no longer has any horticultural pretensions, but is an impenetrable jungle with fronds of barbed brambles clutching at me as I machete my way through to buy vegetables in the nearest supermarket.

45. Something Sensational to Read on the Train

In these days of recession, when bills come buzzing through the letterbox like wasps on a summer evening, I remember the adage, 'Keep a diary and one day it will keep you!' I have kept a diary for many years and thought with pleasure of the steady income it would bring in.

Not so far for this year, when for the first few days I coughed, snuffled and watched *Ben Hur* on telly in the wonderfully centrally heated house of a long-suffering cousin.

Monday.

Very frosty. Think I am sufficiently recovered, so take myself home. Welcomed back to my tiny cot by a rat who behaved with a great deal more savoir-faire than I did. He wiggled his whiskers while calmly observing my hysterics then trotted off and disappeared behind a biscuit tin. When I realized that behaving as a cartoon female by standing on a chair and screaming was not getting me anywhere, I daringly poked the biscuit tin with an umberella but the rat had left that haven for some place unknown. Put rat poison on the windowsill.

Tuesday.

Rat poison has disappeared – is rat now dying behind the cupboard? My meals are very simple with the minimum of preparation, in case the rat leaves its sick bed. Car does not start so cannot escape. Cold water has frozen.

Wednesday.

Did not know what trouble was until today. Car dead – am not sure about rat. This evening, as I am declaiming my sorrows over the telephone, I hear the sound of rushing water. Water is cascading down the wall of the bathroom – I put buckets under it but they fill up in a few seconds – leave them overflowing while I race round outside with torch that needs a new battery, in search of the tap to turn the mains off: find it in a bramble bush, but turn it the wrong way. The neighbours, whom I have summoned, brave the bramble bush and stop the flow of water; they wring out the towels with which I was trying to soak up the flood while I can only wring my hands and weep. The carpet in spare room is under an inch of water and downstairs it is like a monsoon, but miraculously missed the books. Plumber comes.

Friday.

Is the smell in the house damp or dead rat? I can't tell with my cold! Car costs €120.

Hopefully, I look back to last year. Most entries are about whether or not I mowed the lawn or went to Kilkenny and, if so, did I interview bank manager with unsatisfactory outcome. There is a lot about the dog!

Wednesday.

Took the dog along the walk by the river. There was always a path used by the fishermen, but now it has been 'improved' by a FÁS scheme which has put in metal structures like tiger traps over the ditches and streams. Plaques with arrows have been nailed to posts in case I should not be able to find my way along the riverbank. The dog does not follow the arrows but goes after a grey squirrel. I do a lot of calling and whistling before dog returns.

Dinner with the Macnamaras. Decide on warmth and comfort rather than elegance – I am aware that unless I wear purple no one will notice how OAPs like me are dressed.

The other guests, now known to me as Sylvia and Monty, must have been here before as they are also clad for arctic conditions. However, the Macnamaras have turned up their heating and lit huge fires so that I and my fellow guests swelter, our faces scarlet, and gasp for water.

Conversation on the economy – what else is there to talk about? It turns out other guests have, or possibly now had, connections in the financial world and are restive when I tell them how the world should be run.

Thursday.

Why is it that junk mail always looks more entrancing than my mail? Mr Howard Junta wishes to share with me several million pounds that have been left to him by his maternal uncle. This is not the only good fortune that has come my way as I have won many, many millions in a lottery that I have never entered. Leo Foster wants to get to know me better – perhaps after I have taken Viagra, also on offer to me at a Special Price. My own email is one bill and a friend who has changed her email address.

Tuesday.

Oh, my God, today I had to do battle with the two pheasants that have been hanging in my porch. Oh why, oh why do I allow anyone to give me dead pheasants? Why do I even know people who shoot them? Started off by plucking them, but huge hunks of skin came away as well so I ended up skinning them, which is certainly easier. And I cleaned them. Sister-in-law once told me that one can do anything in rubber gloves and it is true. Michael and Jennifer, Gerald Johnson and the Trevors to eat the casserolled pheasants – Michael and Jennifer have been for a cruise up the Nile and by the end of the meal everyone knows exactly what it is like to go on a cruise up the Nile and have each sworn never ever to venture up the Nile in case they find M & J there.

There is a welcome diversion when Gerald bites on some shot and has v. awkward time with his false teeth. I think he hopes that we think they are his own and pretends he is picking up his napkin under the table while he takes them out. The Trevors and I get the giggles, but M & J just think we are amused by their tales of visiting the Valley of the Kings and tell us yet another boring anecdote about suffering from Gippy Tummy.

This can be hardly termed a page-turner and won't make the bestseller lists. Briefly, I consider blackmail: a search reveals an entry written in code and the diary heavily annotated with PRIVATE and what terrible things will happen to those who dare to look inside. The code is not exactly on the Bletchley Park scale where they broke the Enigma Code. I read with interest that on 8 July Michael Healy and I went skinny-dipping. The rest of the diary alas is blank. Vaguely I remember Michael Healy, who lived nearby and was at least two years younger than me. I think he made a career for himself in Bord Bainne. From the date of this disgraceful event, I was eleven at the time. Fear that this youthful indiscretion cannot be relied on to bring in the lolly.

46. *Alone*

Greta Garbo yearned 'to be alone' – a position that I find myself in often, as I am 'an unclaimed treasure', or in other words an elderly spinster. This is a situation that looks like continuing into the foreseeable future. All those dreams of walking hand in hand into the sunset or listening tenderly to the patter of little feet have faded into wistful reverie that is not unmixed with thankfulness.

Now I live alone in a bee-loud glade in a cottage with roses and honeysuckle rampaging round the door. I can do exactly what I like, I can lie abed all day and make gazpacho all night; I can sing in my bath and keep the telephone under the stairs. I haven't got round to living off sardines out of a tin, but I am pretty good at letting old newspapers and dirty mugs pile up around me.

Genesis, chapter 2, says it is not good for man, or in this case woman, to be alone. I am not sure I agree, except when it comes to emptying the garbage, changing a flat tyre, unblocking the gutters or pruning back the honeysuckle and roses (which are shortly going to bring down the roof of the porch), and the other menial tasks that are generally still considered man's work.

Am I ever lonely? Yes, of course I am, but not often as I have very good friends, neighbours and relations who have become accustomed to finding me in their kitchens, reading their newspapers, drinking their coffee and willing to share with them all my little joys and sorrows.

When I first started living alone, those folk who had adopted 'The Good Life' would bring me four-legged companions with whom they had become tired and no longer wished to own – the animal that owners get tired of quickest is a goat! The self-sufficienters wax lyrical about the milk and cheese and how the goat eats brambles: actually, it prefers vegetables, herbaceous borders and trees, especially if they belong to a neighbour. Geese are also often on offer. 'No need for a mower when they are around! And they are really good watchdogs.' What is not described is the huge mess they make everywhere and not only do they scare away potential robbers but also anyone else coming to call.

Am I frightened of robbers? Well, I have passed the stage of listening to them shinning up the drainpipe or scrambling through the bathroom window. No longer do I search under the beds and in the cupboards when I come home late at night. I used to have a pepper pot handy so that I could blind any intruder, but I was never sure of the efficacy of this protection, especially as I would have had to say, 'Stand still so I can aim the pepper into your eyes.' The last time I heard burglars was at 2 am on the gravel below my bedroom. Bravely I crawled to the window and, like Barbara Fritchie, stuck out my old grey head. In the moonless night there appeared to be a good many robbers gathering outside and I quaked in my slippers until there came a friendly moo from the middle of my delphiniums.

When I was new to the job of living alone, there was one very strange occasion when just at midnight the grandfather clock chimed twelve times. The clock had not worked since before I was born. I ran to the telephone to summon the immediate aid of the guards, but then realized that I didn't know how I was going to explain the phenomenon to them, nor what they could do. In the end I retired to my bedroom with the chest of drawers against the door and a book on exorcising ghosts. When I woke in the morning, I, or possibly the ghost, had written on a bit of paper: 'Mem: buy rat poison.'

During the long winter evenings I would like to say I pass the time improving myself, or knitting garments for the poor, but this is seldom the case. I played bridge on the computer until I was expelled for being too slow. Patience, I found, was more my line, but that became such a mania I have kept to my New Year's resolution to quit playing. I don't have a TV otherwise I would have it on night and day. Sometimes, I sit pen in hand waiting for inspiration for my great *oeuvre* but sadly I am soon distracted by the necessity of setting a mousetrap or reading the most unedifying thrillers that I buy in a thrift shop.

In my time I have taken evening classes: what glorious prospects are opened up when one signs up for courses to learn Chinese, car maintenance, or judo – how I longed to surprise my friends by tossing them across the room. I bought all the gear; the white pyjamas, the white belt, tied back my hair and went to the very chilly hall. The first lesson, we did a lot of stamping our bare feet and grunting, which were not at all the skills I needed to improve my social life. During the second lesson, I was retying my belt when a small but stout child, catching me off guard, knocked me to the ground and then proceeded to strangle me. Luckily the instructor saw my purple face and popping eyes before I expired – I never went back. The next year it was Chinese. After three lessons, I could honk and snuffle in what I thought was pretty fluent Mandarin, but when I asked for a bowl of rice in the Flowering Cherry Restaurant, the waiter brought a telephone directory. My car broke down on the way to the class on car maintenance.

Living alone, I am sure, is bad for my character as there is nobody to disagree with my ideas, bad for my appearance as there is no one to tell me when the back of my skirt is tucked into my knickers and bad for my cottage as there is no one but me to clean it. But snuggled up with a peanut butter and jelly sandwich, and a book entitled *How to Win Friends & Influence People*, life is OK.

47. Twelve Days of Christmas

Christmas came early to me this year. My small black spaniel, Inca, her tail wagging like a mad metronome, appeared with what I first took to be an old pillow leaking feathers in her mouth. On closer examination I found it was a turkey, a teenage turkey, which had been snatched from the springtime of its existence by death, or rather by Inca. It required no Sherlock Holmes to detect where the murder had been committed for the terrified siblings of the victim were squawking and gobbling in huddled groups in my neighbour's yard where they were being reared for the Christmas market.

I have to confess that I did contemplate concealing the crime – in fact I tried to dig a grave for the corpse but the excessively dry weather had made the earth rock-hard and I could only scratch a depression on the surface that would scarcely bury a leg let alone a six-pound turkey. I then considered denying all knowledge of the offence, inventing an alibi and imputing the felony to a fox. But there was the possibility of the postman who

had suffered much vociferous displeasure in the past from Inca
coming forward as a hostile witness.

As I cogitated on these matters, I took the disgraced one for
a walk in the fields far, far from the scene of the atrocity. She
scampered gaily along the ditches and returned hoping to assuage
my anger by bringing back a pheasant in her jaws. This was an
even more heinous crime than the turkey as the keepers of game
protect their birds with unparalleled ferocity and even if they
don't shoot you, their language is not nice. This time there was
no wrestling with my conscience as I threw the pheasant into the
hedge and retreated with the utmost speed across country to the
nearest road and then went straight home to hide under my bed.

Inca is, or rather was, a stray I found one morning on my
doorstep, very wet and miserable, her great brown eyes pleading humbly for just a stale crust and a few wisps of straw on
which to sleep. I made strenuous efforts to find an owner. But no
one came forward to claim her. I can now well understand why
and am all for the game laws of the seventeenth century when
the keeping of setters, hounds and spaniels was prohibited for
persons with an income of less than £100 per annum.

She inserted herself into the household and, once established,
oh, how her demands changed. Luxuriating in the best armchair,
she disdained crusts and dined only on expensive dog food.

How much she would have enjoyed the life of Lady Dapper
and Miss Kitsy, the two spaniels whom Ned Eyre, an eighteenth-
century eccentric, adopted as daughters and co-heiresses. Dinner
was served every day at one o'clock and, for Lady Dapper and
Miss Kitsy, there was either a fat duck hot from the spit or a
tender chicken with sippets. The rest of the party was not so
lucky as Ned Eyre only liked very plain food and there was an
almighty row when an elderly lady was caught stealing the leg of
a duck from Lady Dapper. Once, travelling to Galway, Ned had
his carriage filled with the finest ripe peaches and apricots for

Lady Dapper while poor Miss Kitsy and his human companions had to make to do with inferior fruit. With this diet, it is not surprising that when the party called in on Ardfry House, Lady Dapper should dirty the carpet. Unfortunately, Lord Louth who was staying in the house and had poor eyesight, stepped in the mess when he was on his way to his daughter's wedding.

I am not so indulgent with Inca, but did think that swimming in the river would be a harmless exercise; not so – her eye has been caught by the two geese that live on the opposite bank. I know just what the recipient of all those gifts for the twelve days of Christmas must have felt!

48. *A Long Illness Bravely Borne*

When the radiologist said 'God love you', I knew I had cancer, and when the doctor said 'Grim news', I knew I was going to die. I told my brother where I had hidden the silver teapot and that there was an open tin of dog food in the fridge. He, though sympathetic about my imminent demise, considered it unlikely that I would be whisked up to heaven immediately and that, with present-day medicine, I still had a good chance of reaching my nineties. This was a relief, as I was unsure I wanted to renew my acquaintance with the loved ones who had gone before. Would I be greeted at the Pearly Gates by Aunt Bertha, never my favourite but so kind? The thought of her floating about on a cloud with a harp has caused me an unresolved crisis of belief.

I was afraid of the future – or, rather, no future – but I realized that any leave-taking would be very much easier for me than for others, as I have neither a husband nor what the taxman calls dependents.

I made a mental list of what I would be relieved to leave

behind, starting with grand notions such as most contemporary Irish architecture, too many people in the world and the consequences of global warming, but deeper deliberation made me pleased at the thought of being parted from the kitchen drain, never having to buy shoes again and – the most positive advantage – not growing old to suffer loneliness and physical deterioration. What was I going to miss? All the things I had meant to do and never got round to achieving, my Special Savings Account coming to fruition and, of course, life itself.

But friends, neighbours, relations and sleeping pills meant I had remarkably few moments to brood on my sad lot. During the following weeks I felt like a debutante. The telephone never stopped ringing, invitations poured in, visitors came to see me. Most of them urged me to be positive. I was not sure how to carry out this instruction. I tried using it as a mantra, murmuring 'Be positive, be positive, be positive' while I sat in the doctor's waiting room. I sounded like Thomas the Tank Engine, and, even though there were fewer chairs than people waiting, all the seats cleared round me. So I stopped muttering and went back to reading *Hello!* magazine, the favourite periodical in waiting rooms (it should be possible to gauge people's health by their knowledge of Posh and Becks).

I did not suffer much pain or discomfort from a mastectomy, though I found it difficult to spell, but, like a fairy-tale princess, I was told never to prick my finger and to garden with gloves, as the healing abilities of my right arm have been impaired.

My well-wishers proffered alternative cures. I gave up dairy products, which course of action apparently had miraculously healed some sufferers, and it did make me feel that I was doing something active to help with the treatment. A friend made me drink elderberry juice, which, like the witches in *Macbeth*, she had stirred and incanted over as it bubbled on the stove. It was so nasty that one felt it must be doing good.

I had chemotherapy in a nearby hospital. The treatment was not as bad as I had imagined – or perhaps the elderberry juice counteracted it. Every three weeks I would go into the hospital and lie on a bed, reading a book on dinosaurs. I don't know how I came to choose dinosaurs, which, being extinct, are not a very positive subject.

The chemo made me sick immediately afterwards, but otherwise did not devastate me as it does many people. Although I live by myself, kind friends and neighbours dropped by or stayed if I was feeling fragile. I think they envisaged smoothing snowy pillows, concocting tisanes and arranging the flowers; they were not so excited when I required their help with digging out the recalcitrant drain.

Often I forgot how ill I could have been, and when people took my hand in both of theirs, looked deep into my eyes and asked me how I truly was, only to hear that I felt fine, they emitted the slightest frisson of disappointment.

My goddaughter cut off my hair when it started to fall out, then took me to Dublin to choose a wig. She steered me firmly from the long blonde one I had pounced on, hoping it would restore me to youth and beauty; nor would she let me even try on a fringed raven-black hairpiece that, combined with a long cigarette holder, would, I was sure, turn me into a fascinating femme fatale. The wig that was chosen looked like a mop, but I was assured it was the same as my late, lamented hair. Later I found another wig in the dressing-up box which, though on the large side with waves and curls like the Judge's in *Alice's Adventures in Wonderland*, I fancied for social occasions. I gave enormous pleasure to the congregation at a wedding when I wore it with a Russian fur hat perched on top. The edifice slipped from my head and under the pew as I knelt to pray. 'I told you the wig we bought was a better fit,' said the goddaughter, censoriously.

Having come through chemotherapy, radiotherapy was a

doddle, with plenty of time to study the Beckhams' lifestyle, for one spent a long time just waiting. Otherwise I was able to enjoy Dublin – slipping past the gatekeeper at night after the theatre was like being a student again.

Two years on I feel remarkably well, and my hair is so thick that my hairdresser is earning a fortune. Am I still frightened? Yes. I go through periods of confidence, then something very slight will cast a shadow in the corner of my mind. But I am still here, and so is the kitchen drain.

49. *Cancer Clocks*

The clock on the mantelpiece had stopped at twenty-five to three: the battery must have run out. By a coincidence the time-piece on the computer had gone haywire, perhaps there had been a power failure when I had been abroad earlier in the summer. And I have to do a calculation whenever I look at my wrist-watch – on the plane coming back from holidays, I set it forwards instead of back – I keep meaning to put it right but I haven't, and I have not yet read the instruction book in the car as to how to alter the hands of the clock from summer to winter time.

Now I am glad because I do not want to watch time ticking away into the past and there does not seem as if there is going to be a future, or not that I can envisage except as little pink clouds with people sitting around in their nightdresses. I am not so eager to join even my nearest and dearest, twanging away on a harp for eternity, which must pall. I will probably end up with Veronica Cave whose death made a great impact on me in my second year at school. Not that I really knew her because she was three years above me; she had upbraided me twice for running along the passages and once she had commended me for hitting a goal from mid-field. But when the headmistress had broken the news of her death, my tears had been copious and for a long time I believed that she interceded on my behalf in difficult situations, though, with her gymslip and lumpy figure, she seems now to be rather an unlikely guardian angel.

Looking back, not at memories that play like familiar videos but at a series of vignettes that spring complete with all the senses – there seems no rhyme or reason for them – they are neither happy nor sad. A pile of stones by the roadside – there is a magnificent view as a backcloth because I know where the stones are, but I do not see it. The hot glare of the sun is draining the colour and mystery from the grass and leaves round the heap by the side of the road, leaving them dry and dusty.

In another place, another country, my Aunt, whistling that bit from the *Pastoral Symphony*, walks past the blobs of Michaelmas daisies in the border. The September evening is already sharp and she is on her way to put away the trowel and fork with which she has been working.

I should be measuring time, not squandering it.

'Ah, fill the cup: what boots it to repeat how time is slipping underneath our feet.' A mantra to use while I wait for the time check on the radio –

50. *Hymns Ancient & Modern*

I am not looking forward to the journey from this Vale of Tears to that Happy Land far, far away, as detailed by *Hymns Ancient & Modern*. The call o'er the tumult of our life's wild restless sea sounds most unenticing, more like navigating the Irish Channel. And I am one of those timorous mortals, who start and shrink to cross the narrow sea and linger, shivering on the brink at the sight of the hungry billow curling. But no doubt I will be driven by storm and flood from my bourne of time and place so hope that there will be some moaning at the bar when I put out to sea, especially when they hear me crying from the deep where the vessels are being tempest-tossed midst rocks and mists and quicksands.

Hymn singers are familiar with the nautical way of life, for they have long wondered if their anchors will hold in the straits of fear when the breakers have told that the reef is near and have suffered other perils of the ocean, such as dark rude waters, restless waves, not to mention rock and tempest, fire and foe. Landlubbers, too, have not had an easy time finding their way to

Jordan's bank. The road being long and dreary and its ending out of sight and the burning of the noonday heat on this barren land makes the way very drear. Our hearts are filled with sadness for we have lost the way. At this moment, I am sure the child she-bear will appear for we are oft in danger, oft in woe.

There is no need to ask: are we weak and heavy-laden, cumbered with a load of care? For we have to carry that very awkward moving tent o'er moor and fen, o'er crag and torrent and the trivial round the common task includes pitching it nightly. No wonder our couch is wet with tears and we long for a kindly light amid the encircling gloom.

Is it going to be worth all this wrestling on to Heaven 'gainst storm and wind and tide? For on Caanan's happy shore all the saints are knitting, which is not my idea of paradise! Alternatively, it may be like a prep school with a noble army, men and boys, the matron and the maid, gathered there.

At least there will be happy retribution, short toil, eternal rest – but when? For there is no night in heaven, no cloud or passing vapour dims the brightness of the air, endless noonday, glorious noonday from the sun of suns is there. And the noise! It is not going to be easy to get any sleep for, hark, ten thousand voices sounding far and wide throughout the sky, hallelujah is the anthem ever dear to choirs on high that are accompanied by harp and lute, loud trumpets and bright clarions, and the gentle soothing flute. Less musical are the shouts of praise that cleave the sky; cherubims answering seraphims and circling planets singing on their way. Those in search of the silence of eternity may wish to bid the cruel discord cease.

Of course, it is a land of pure delight with never-wilting flowers; there are pleasant pastures, verdant fields where sweetest herbage grows. In *Hymns Ancient & Modern*, they do say, knowledge of that life is small, but many authors predict we will be sheep – a crowd of frightened sheep till we are found wandering in the dark, brought to the safety of the fold and enjoined to 'Sing ye little flock'. This metamorphosis would explain the knitting, but I wonder how we will wear the golden crowns.